Fanatical About Football

FANATICAL ABOUT FOOTBALL

YOU MUST REMEMBER THIS . . .

EDITED BY JEFF CONNOR

BELL'S
SCOTTISH FOOTBALL LEAGUE

MAINSTREAM
PUBLISHING

EDINBURGH AND LONDON

First published in Great Britain in 2003 by
MAINSTREAM PUBLISHING (EDINBURGH) LTD
7 Albany Street
Edinburgh EH1 3UG

ISBN 1 84018 787 5

A catalogue record for this book is available from the British Library

Typeset in Janson Text and Univers

Printed in Great Britain by
Butler & Tanner Ltd, Frome and London

ACKNOWLEDGEMENTS

Sincere thanks go to all the contributors who gave time, energy and memories so readily; it was a joy and privilege to talk to all of them. This book would not have reached fruition without BELL'S® and Euro RSCG Leedex, whose support was invaluable. I would also like to thank Lord Macfarlane for agreeing to write a foreword and to all at Mainstream Publishing, in particular Bill Campbell, Peter MacKenzie, Will Mackie, Tina Hudson and Graeme Blaikie. The input and support from numerous newspaper picture desks, particularly the *Daily Record*, was generous and unstinting.

Last, but by no means least, Frances Rendall and Fiona Ross worked wonders on the transcripts and took an enormous amount of pressure off my shoulders.

CONTENTS

FOREWORD

As the UK's number one whisky, BELL'S® has its roots firmly in Scotland. We are proud to support Scottish football and privileged to be part of the sports success story.

BELL'S are long-time supporters of Scottish football, having pioneered the sponsorship of the League Cup more than 20 years ago, the BELL'S League Championship in the mid-'90s and currently as sponsors of the Scottish Football League and the BELL'S Cup.

Up to 40 of the finest quality malts from the 4 main whisky-producing regions of Scotland go into BELL'S; the result is a successful combination, not unlike BELL'S and Scottish football – it's all in the blend!

We are delighted to be involved in such a passionate sport and wanted to bring this to life in a way which would benefit the future of Scottish football.

What could be better than a book which captures the exhilaration and sentiments of our national game, past and present, as well as generating money which will be invested into developing the game.

Fanatical About Football includes tales of famous matches, spectacular goals and the teams and characters at the clubs. It is an indispensable look at the joys and occasional despairs of Scottish football.

On behalf of BELL'S I'd like to thank the many people who have contributed to this book, from politicians, authors, artists, players past and present and loyal fans. We would also like to say thanks for all the photographs, which have kindly been gifted by clubs across Scotland as well as newspapers and sports agencies.

Finally, and perhaps most importantly, I'd also like to take this opportunity to thank you for buying this book, all royalties of which will be invested into the future development of Scottish football.

Lord Macfarlane of Bearsden, KT
Honorary Life President of BELL'S

INTRODUCTION

During the course of the 41 interviews undertaken for this book I lost count of the times that the person seated opposite me said: football has been my life. It is an old cliché, but in many cases among the men and women I spoke to, it was, literally, the truth.

And here is the common theme and the justification for this book: that football in Scotland can take over a psyche and reduce grown adults to tears of frustration and disappointment or lift them to exultation to a quite unreasonable extent. In the case of football played at the level below the small segment that is the Scottish Premier League (SPL), the main emotions remain those of expectation followed by a sort of temporary mortification and, if nothing else, working on this book illustrated, to paraphrase Hemingway, the adage that man (substitute football fan) can be defeated, but not destroyed. The faithful who follow East Stirlingshire, Queen of the South, Alloa Athletic and even, at a higher level, Falkirk, St Johnstone and the Edinburgh and Dundee clubs will surely agree with this, for while all have enjoyed success within their own definition of that word, the fans of every club in Scotland have at times required a resilience above and beyond the call of duty.

The common language throughout this book is football and it

is the reason why the mascot of Dunfermline Athletic finds himself in a forum alongside the first minister of Scotland and a Hollywood film star. It is why a description of a *local derby* between Stranraer and Queen of the South is next to recollections of a Scotland victory at Wembley and why a part-timer from Queen's Park is rubbing shoulders in these pages with Dave Mackay, Lawrie Reilly and Ally McCoist.

The love of football and a club may be an unexplored tangibility, but I hope that after reading this we may be able to understand what makes people devote a large proportion of their lives to the spectacle of a round ball being pursued by a group of adult males in shorts and stockings.

The chapters are self-explanatory. 'Home' deals with the first stirrings within the breasts of young football fans, their family connections and first visits to their local club. 'Stargazing' is all about favourite players and '90 Minutes', notable matches. 'Boss', Chapter Four, examines those strange creatures who sit in the dug-out and the manager's office for most of their waking hours and 'Faces in the Crowd' is devoted to the lifeblood of the game, the fans, and their eccentricities. I have left the contributors to speak for themselves although, because some football managers are earthy and outspoken types, some discreet editing was necessary on occasion.

Five themes, then, but presented by forty-one people for whom the description Fanatical about Football defines them totally.

Jeff Connor,
Edinburgh, August 2003

THE CAST

PATRICK BARCLAY was born in London but transported to Dundee at an early age where he began a lifelong love affair with the Dark Blues. He saw his first match at Dens Park in 1957 and, although now living and working in London, that initial passion has never waned through Dundee's greatest victories in Europe, the trauma of the departure of Alan Gilzean to Tottenham Hotspur and the 2003 Scottish Cup defeat to Rangers at Hampden Park, a fixture that Paddy managed to convince his boss required some in-depth colour from a *neutral* source. Paddy is the chief football writer of the *Sunday Telegraph* and appears regularly on television.

IAN BLACK hails from Dalbeattie in Dumfriesshire and his devotion to Queen of the South has seen him dress up as the club mascot, Dougie the Doonhamer, paint the Palmerston Park stand, mend fences and collect litter. He is also curator of the club museum, which can boast a Zico jersey, and acts as the club tour guide. Ian is 37, married to Rosa and has two daughters, Natasha and Vanessa, both of whom are season ticket holders.

CRAIG BROWN is one of three brothers born to an RAF officer and former professional footballer. A trained PE teacher, with degrees in geography and art, he signed for Glasgow Rangers at the age of 17 before moving on to Dundee where he made his name as a feisty wing-half. A serious knee injury played havoc with his playing career, however, and after a spell as a part-timer he moved into management with Clyde and Motherwell. One of Alex Ferguson's deputies with Scotland at the 1986 World Cup in Mexico, Craig took over as international manager in 1993, guiding Scotland to the World Cup finals in 1998 and achieving European Championship qualification in 1996. He stepped down in October 2001, and succeeded David Moyes as team manager of Preston North End. He now lives in north Lancashire.

GORDON BROWN has been Member of Parliament for Dunfermline East since 1983 and Chancellor of the Exchequer since 1997. Born in 1951 in Fife and educated at Kirkcaldy High School and Edinburgh University, where he gained First Class Honours and then a Doctorate, the Chancellor is an avid Raith Rovers fan and a self-confessed member of the Tartan Army. Happy to admit that he stayed off school for the day when Scotland had to beat Italy to qualify for the World Cup finals in England in 1966, he has followed his country at home and abroad ever since, through thick and thin, in between pursuing one of the most successful political careers of modern times. His boyhood hero was Jim Baxter, a player he first saw at Stark's Park as a schoolboy. Outside football, he lists his other interests as tennis and film.

TERRY CHRISTIE, who is now in his fifth decade in the game, is one of Scotland's most underrated managers and has enjoyed success with Newtongrange Star, Stenhousemuir, Meadowbank Thistle and now Alloa. Born in Edinburgh in 1943, Terry has earned himself the nickname of 'The Duffle' because of a lucky coat he wears, a nickname that has even inspired the title of a website. He has taken Alloa to promotion twice and inspired them to win the BELL'S Challenge Cup final in 2000, the first major trophy for the club. Resolutely part-time throughout his football career, Terry retired as headmaster of Musselburgh Grammar School in 2003.

STUART COSGROVE, if not the most famous St Johnstone fan in Britain, is certainly the most high-profile, and during countless TV and radio appearances has never failed to sing the praises of his beloved Saints. Born on a Perth housing scheme overlooking both of St Johnstone's grounds, Muirton Park and McDiarmid Park, Stuart claims his allegiance was pre-ordained when he was christened Stuart John Francis Cosgrove (St Johnstone Football Club). In real life Stuart is head of programmes (nations and regions) for Channel 4, based in Glasgow, and still finds the energy to follow Saints, write a newspaper column and present Radio Scotland's true-fan phone-in show *Off the Ball*. Stuart is also an honorary professor at the University of Stirling and the author of the highly acclaimed *Hampden Babylon: Sex and Scandal in Scottish Football*.

BOB CRAMPSEY was born within 200 yards of Hampden Park on the South Side of Glasgow in 1930. He is one of the most respected sports commentators in Scotland and his acute observations on football and cricket have found a wide audience on both radio and television and in newspapers. In many ways the sporting equivalent of Memory Man Leslie Welch, Bob Crampsey has an encyclopaedic knowledge of sporting facts and figures and has witnessed most of the great football occasions in Scotland.

He attended Holyrood Secondary School, Glasgow University and the Royal College of Music before moving into a career teaching history and administering schools. Bob claims he heard an early programme on STV and in typically modest manner said: 'I could do better.' He is still doing better at the age of 73.

PETER DONALD is the secretary of the Scottish Football League (SFL), and was born in Johnstone, Renfrewshire on 8 August 1950. A self-confessed midfielder of modest skills in his youth, Peter channelled his love of the game in other directions, supporting his local team Johnstone Burgh and eventually moving into administration, first with the Scottish Football Association (SFA) and then with the League. Peter took over his current duties at Hampden Park 14 years ago when Jim Farry moved from the SFL to the SFA and claims that it was 'me plus cash for Farry'.

JULIE FLEETING is 22 years old and is the captain of Scotland's women's football team. Her family background is steeped in the game as father Jim managed Kilmarnock and is now head of the SFA Community Programme. Julie initially played for a local boys' club before moving to Ayr United ladies' team and San Diego Spirit in California, where she has proved a resounding success. She is known in the Women's United Soccer Association (WUSA) as 'Air Scotland' for her heading ability and regularly plays in front of 7,000-plus crowds.

BRIAN FLYNN was born in Falkirk in 1957, the year, as he is at pains to point out, Falkirk last won the Scottish Cup. Brian also admits that he saw the club's second attempt, 40 years later in 1997, so has still to see his side actually win it. Brian is part-owner of the well-known Falkirk pub/restaurant Behind the Wall and accepted the award for Football Supporters' Pub of the Year in 2002–03. Behind the Wall also supports the other local clubs Stenhousemuir, Stirling Albion and East Stirlingshire.

RICHARD GORDON joined BBC Scotland's sports department in October 1991 after working in a bank and then branching out into broadcasting via hospital radio, Northsound in Aberdeen and the Glasgow-based Radio Clyde. Born in Aberdeen in 1960, his main role is presenter of *Sportsound* on Radio Scotland, but he is also on the presenters' rota for BBC Scotland's *Sportscene* and has worked as reporter, presenter and commentator on a number of TV and radio programmes covering football, golf, rugby and boxing. He was educated at Skene Square Primary, Aberdeen Grammar School and Aberdeen College of Commerce and lists his main interests as reading, listening to music, skiing, golf, scuba diving, amateur dramatics and travel.

ALLAN GRIEVE is a head teacher at Falkirk High School, and was born in Perth in August 1960. Allan began a lifelong association with Stirling Albion in the mid-'60s and has seen the club through most of its good and lean times, both at the old ground of Annfield and at its current headquarters at Forthbank. He has fulfilled many roles for Stirling Albion, and even sat on the bench as a substitute in a reserve team game one never-to-be-forgotten night.

LAURA HIRD was born in 1966 within a stone's throw of Tynecastle and it was inevitable that football would play some part in her life. The only child of a storeman and a secretary, Laura went to Tynecastle High School and after an erratic career course that included packing coleslaw, selling classical records and working for a bookies, she took a course in contemporary writing at Middlesex Polytechnic (and lived close by Arsenal's ground at Highbury). She received a Scottish Arts Council bursary in 1997 to allow her to write full-time and was picked for Rebel Inc. editor Kevin Williamson's stellar team for the short story collection *Children of Albion Rovers*. Her novel *Born Free* was shortlisted for the 2000 Whitbread First Novel Award.

JOHN HUGHES has earned undying fame as one of Scotland's most whole-hearted players with Berwick Rangers, Falkirk, Celtic and Hibs, and is one of the great characters of Scottish football. Born the son of a dock worker in Leith in September 1964, 'Yogi' has remained totally committed to his roots and is arguably the most recognisable face in his native town. He is now player-manager of Falkirk.

JOHN LAMBIE, who was born in Whitburn, West Lothian, is known as 'Mr Partick Thistle' after three spells with the Firhill club, but he has also worked at Hibs, Hamilton Accies and Falkirk. John, in fact, began his professional playing career with Falkirk before moving to St Johnstone where he captained the side in Europe. His career in management has been defined not only by success – he inspired Hamilton to a famous cup win over Rangers and has never been sacked – but also by a frightening commitment and candour. A fly-on-the-wall TV documentary cemented John's place in football folklore, confirming that this is a man who throughout his life has eaten and breathed the game.

JIM LEISHMAN is now general manager at Dunfermline Football Club after a three-year spell in charge of Livingston which saw the West Lothian club reach the SPL for the first time in their short history. Jim was also manager of Dunfermline for seven years and took his hometown club from the Third Division to the top division. Born in Lochgelly, eight miles from Dunfermline, in 1953, Jim was a stout defender for the Pars and Cowdenbeath before a broken leg ended a promising career. One of the most colourful characters in the Scottish game, Jim is a noted after-dinner speaker and won fame (some would say notoriety) as the Poet Laureate of Football because of his habit of summarising games in rhyme.

CRAIG LEVEIN was born in Dunfermline in October 1964, and was brought up in Aberdour. He attended Inverkeithing High School, where he played in the same school team as Gordon Durie, and played juvenile football for Dalgety Bay and Leven

Royals before joining Inverkeithing Under-16s and Lochore Juniors. Soon to become one of Scotland's most cultured defenders, Craig joined Cowdenbeath in 1981 and signed for Hearts two years later. During a 14-year career, and despite interruptions through injury, he won 16 caps in all for his country and played in the 1990 World Cup finals in Italy. Injury finally curtailed his career at the age of 31 and he moved into management with his first club, Cowdenbeath, before succeeding Jim Jefferies at Tynecastle. Craig quickly made a name as one of the brightest young managers in the Scottish game and Hearts finished third in the SPL in 2002–03.

LORD MACFARLANE OF BEARSDEN, KT, is honorary life president of Macfarlane Group PLC. Born in Glasgow in 1926, he joined the board of Guinness PLC in September 1986 and worked his way up to chairman. In 1996 he retired from the post and was appointed honorary life president.

Lord Macfarlane is married with one son and four daughters and lives in Bearsden, Glasgow. As life-long president of BELL'S, both Lord Macfarlane and his wife Lady Macfarlane are regular visitors to Scottish football matches, travelling to every single Scottish Football league ground each season. Educated at the High School of Glasgow, he was knighted in December 1992 for his services to industry and arts and elevated to the Peerage in 1991. He is acknowledged as a leading patron of the arts in Scotland and has been chairman of the Fine Arts Society since 1976 and life president since 1999. Other positions held include the Lord High Commissioner to the General Assembly of the Church of Scotland in 1992, 1993 and 1997, as well as patron of the Scottish Licensed Trade Association.

DAVE MACKAY is one of Britain's greatest post-war players and a genuine legend of the game. His stature as a warrior-like wing-half and fearless leader for Hearts and Spurs is indisputable. Dave was born in Edinburgh in November 1934, and played in a Hearts side which contained Willie Bauld and Alfie Conn from 1952 until 1959. Spurs manager Bill Nicholson paid Hearts £32,000 for him in 1959 and he went on to make 318 appearances for the London club, including the Double season of 1960–61. Two broken legs interfered with Dave's Scotland career but he still won 22 caps before going on to manage Swindon, Nottingham Forest, Derby, Walsall and Birmingham. He lives in Nottingham.

FORDYCE MAXWELL is the oldest of a family of nine and was brought up on a small tenanted farm in the Borders at Coldstream. A lifelong Berwick Rangers supporter, Fordyce attended agricultural college but instead of becoming a farmer went into journalism on a farming magazine. He joined the *Scotsman* for the first time in 1969, was there for eight years, and then went back into farming for twelve years in between freelance writing assignments. He rejoined the *Scotsman* in 1989 and has been the widely respected farming and rural affairs editor since.

FRANK McAVEETY was born in Glasgow in 1962, and obtained a BA Joint Honours (English and history) at Strathclyde University in 1983. Initially a secondary school teacher from 1984 to 1998, Frank was also involved in local government in his home city and in 1997 became the youngest-ever leader of the council. Still finding time to support Celtic, he was elected MSP for Glasgow Shettleston in May 1999 and served in the Scottish Executive from July 1999 until October 2000 as deputy minister for local government. In 2003 he was appointed to the position of minister for tourism, culture and sport in the Scottish Executive.

JACK McCONNELL is Scotland's first minister. He was born in 1960 and grew up on a sheep farm on the island of Arran. He was educated at Arran High School, Lamlash, then went on to gain a BSc Dip. Ed. at the University of Stirling where he was also president of the Students' Association. A maths teacher for nine years from 1983 and a member of Stirling District Council between 1984 and 1992, Jack McConnell's first involvement with football was as a supporter of Greenock Morton and he has remained an avid follower of the Scotland team. He was appointed Labour's environmental affairs spokesperson for the 1999 Scottish election where he was returned as MSP for Motherwell and Wishaw. He served as finance minister and then education minister before becoming Scotland's third first minister in November 2001. After the 2003 election he was again nominated by the parliament to hold the post. Jack McConnell is married to Bridget and has a daughter and a son. He enjoys listening to music, playing golf and, of course, watching football.

DAVID McGREGOR completed six years as chairman of Forfar Athletic in 2003 and has been secretary since 1983. Born in Dundee in 1950, David moved to Forfar when he was two days old. He edited the programme from 1974 until two seasons ago and also follows most of Scotland's away games.

WILLIE McKIE AND GEORGE ORMISTON have, in some capacity, been involved with Alloa Athletic for most of their lives and are both directors. George, whose father was a director before him, was born in the town in 1930 and his first post was as club treasurer in 1957. He has looked after the club's financial affairs ever since and is now honorary president.

Willie McKie grew up in Newton Stewart in Wigtownshire but arrived in Alloa in 1947, when his father moved the family to a farm in West Fife. He began his unpaid labours at Recreation Park as an eight-year-old, running baths for the players and cleaning boots and since then has been groundsman, chief steward, programme editor and commercial manager. He was also chairman for two years, during which time, he is keen to stress, 'Alloa won a National Cup'!

ALEX McLEISH crowned a coruscating first decade in management when he won the Treble with Rangers in 2002–03 after a remarkable finale to the SPL season. Born in Glasgow in 1959, McLeish began his playing career in 1976 with Aberdeen, where he formed one of the most formidable defensive partnerships in Scottish football history with Willie Miller under the management of Alex Ferguson. McLeish was the bedrock of an Aberdeen team which not only broke the duopoly of the Old Firm (Scottish Premier League Championships in 1980, 1984 and 1985, Scottish Cups in 1982–84, 1986 and 1990 and League Cup in 1986 and 1990), but also made an indelible mark in Europe. Their 2–1 Cup-Winners' Cup win over Real Madrid in Gothenburg in 1983 remains one of Scottish club football's definitive nights. McLeish's 77 caps for Scotland, including three World Cup finals between 1982 and 1990, made him the third most-capped player in the history of the domestic game and in 1990 was voted Scottish Player of the Year. In 1994 he took over as player-manager at Motherwell, guiding the unfashionable Lanarkshire side to second place in the Premier League the following year before moving to Edinburgh and Easter Road. Under his guidance, Hibs returned to the Premier League and reached the semi-finals of the Scottish Cup in 2000.

ERIC MILLIGAN is a former Lord Provost of Edinburgh and probably Scotland's most high-profile Hearts supporter, a badge he bears with some pride. Born and brought up in Gorgie in the 1950s, Eric attended Tynecastle School and as a young boy was taken by his father to see Hearts' Scottish Cup final win over Celtic in 1956. The love affair with the Jambos goes on. Eric became a regional councillor in 1978, convener of Lothian Regional Council in 1990 and Lord Provost in 1996.

ARTHUR MONTFORD was born in 1939, and although his birthplace was Shawlands in Glasgow, he was brought up in Greenock, went to school in Greenock and has supported

Morton for most of his life. A director of the club, Arthur earned immortality as a sports-jacketed presenter with the original *Scotsport* and as an erudite commentator on the game. A friend and confidant of many managers and players, notably the late Jock Stein, Arthur now lives in Kirkintilloch, and still does occasional radio work.

DAVID MOYES crowned 2002–03, his first full season in charge at Everton, by being voted the Premiership's top manager – ahead of Sir Alex Ferguson and Arsène Wenger – by his fellow managers and a panel of Sky television pundits. The Goodison Park side, for so long Merseyside's 'other' team, finished eighth in the table and at one stage threatened to overhaul arch-rivals Liverpool.

Born in 1963 in Glasgow, Moyes joined Celtic as a junior in January 1980, where his biggest influence was the great full-back Danny McGrain. He began a long career with Preston North End in 1993, making 142 appearances for the north Lancashire club, becoming their manager in 1998. The following year he took Preston into the Second Division play-offs, saw them crowned champions in 2000 and lost the First Division play-off final in 2001 before taking over from Walter Smith at Everton. His prize asset at Goodison Park has proven to be the England starlet Wayne Rooney, but his cult-hero status among Evertonians has been his ability to maintain success with little money and average talent.

BILL PATERSON, one of Scotland's best-known character actors, was born in 1945 in Dennistoun in the East End of Glasgow, within earshot of Celtic Park. After a three-year apprenticeship as a quantity surveyor he took a course at the Royal Scottish Academy of Music and Drama in Renfrew Street, Glasgow, and his first professional acting appearance was with the famed Citizens Theatre in the Gorbals, in their 1967 production of Bertolt Brecht's *Arturo Ui*. After spells with the Citz as actor and assistant director, he became a founding member of John McGrath's 7:84 Company and toured extensively throughout Scotland, Ireland and Europe. His television work includes leading roles in *Wives and Daughters*, *The Crow Road* and *Traffik*, while notable big-screen appearances include parts in *Sunshine*, *The Killing Fields*, *Defence of the Realm* and *Truly, Madly, Deeply*. Bill is married to the theatre and opera designer Hildegard Bechtler. The couple have a son and daughter and live in north London.

IAIN PAXTON made 36 appearances for Scotland as a rugby player between 1981 and 1988 and is now coach of Premiership champions Boroughmuir. An executive with Scottish Mutual in Edinburgh, Iain was born in Dunfermline in 1957, but declined to follow the Pars and instead formed a lifelong allegiance to Raith Rovers.

CHARLIE REID, along with his twin brother Craig, achieved overnight fame with a famous TV appearance on *The Tube*, performing 'Letter From America'. Since then The Proclaimers, as they were christened on their founding in 1983, have achieved international celebrity with their acoustic energy and passionate songwriting. Their debut album, *This is the Story*, went gold and they followed that success with *Sunshine On Leith* in 1988, which became a two-million seller. More albums and worldwide tours followed and they made short work of conquering the notoriously tough American market with 'I'm Gonna Be (500 Miles)' which reached No. 1 in many states. Their latest album, *Born Innocent*, was released in 2003.

The twins' other constant passion, however, has remained football and in particular Hibernian FC.

Both are season ticket holders and Charlie can be regularly spotted at Easter Road with wife Carol and sons Daniel, 11, Sean, 16, and Michael, 7.

LAWRIE REILLY was born in 1928 in Edinburgh and earned undying fame as a member of the Famous Five forward line of Hibs that terrorised Scottish defences in the 1950s. An astute and committed goalscorer, Lawrie was a one-club man, spent 13 years with Hibs and is still the most capped player in the club's history. His goalscoring feats made him popular with fans everywhere and he earned the nickname 'Last Minute Reilly' for his uncanny ability to win or save a match in the dying minutes. Lawrie scored 22 goals in 38 full internationals, a better average than both Denis Law and Kenny Dalglish, and had an amazing 18 hat-tricks for Hibs.

DOUGRAY SCOTT has become one of the country's best-known stage and screen actors through roles in *Regeneration*, *Deep Impact*, *Ever After*, *Gregory's Two Girls*, *Arabian Nights*, *Mission Impossible II* and *Enigma*. Born Stephen Scott in Dunfermline, he was educated in Glenrothes before attending the Welsh College of Music and Drama where he was named most promising drama student. He adopted his grandmother's surname as his first name because his own had already been registered with the actors' union Equity. He began his acting career working in regional theatre, but got his break in 1995 with a part in the ITV drama *Soldier, Soldier*. Subsequently he has appeared in several other TV roles, including an adaptation of Iain Banks' *The Crow Road*. Despite his Fife birthright, Dougray, who is married with twins and lives in London, is a Hibs season ticket holder.

GORDON SHERRY was tipped for a bright golfing future when the 6ft 8in. Kilmarnock lad won the 1995 British Amateur Championship. Gordon duly left Tiger Woods trailing in his wake as he claimed fourth place at Carnoustie in the Scottish Open and played a key role in helping Great Britain and Ireland beat the US in the Walker Cup at Porthcawl. He turned pro in 1996, and is a touring professional at Loch Lomond. Gordon, a fervent Killie fan, is married to Alison and the couple live with their son Thomas, six, and daughter Anna, one, in Helensburgh.

ALEX SMITH was born in December 1939, in the mining village of Cowie, Stirlingshire. A lifelong friend of Billy Bremner, who was raised a few miles away on Stirling's Raploch scheme, Smith was signed by Kilmarnock from the Stirlingshire juvenile team Gowan Hill in 1958, and went on to play for Stenhousemuir, Stirling Albion, East Stirlingshire and Albion Rovers. His first managerial post was at Stenhousemuir in 1969 and five years later he returned to Stirling Albion. The club won the Second Division in 1977, spent four years in the First Division and went into the record books with a 20–0 Scottish Cup victory over Selkirk in 1984.

Smith's most remarkable feats as a manager, however, came in the four years between 1986 and 1990 when he won Scottish Cups with St Mirren and Aberdeen. The fickleness of life as a football manager was perfectly illustrated when he was sacked by Aberdeen in 1991 and Dundee United in 2002. Six weeks later, Alex Smith arrived at Dingwall, where Ross County's youth development scheme has swiftly become the envy of Scottish football and where the man himself still flourishes after over five decades in the game.

SAMMY THE TAMMY was 'born' in 1995 and is well known as Dunfermline's mascot – a large bear noted for his innovative pre-match routines. These have included the firing of a toy cannon for a friendly with Arsenal and a striptease to the tunes from *The Full Monty*. He has been voted Scotland's best match mascot by the BBC. His identity remains a closely guarded secret, although he does admit to being a member of the Tartan Army and a regular traveller away with Scotland in his other guise . . . as a human.

ALEX TOTTEN, one of Scotland's most celebrated managers, was born in February 1946 in Stirlingshire and is now director of football at Falkirk. A former sales manager of the year, Alex is better known for his football exploits. As a full-back he signed as a schoolboy for Bill Shankly at Liverpool, joined the other Shankly at Dundee and also played in the same Falkirk team as Alex Ferguson. His managerial career took him to St Johnstone, Kilmarnock and Falkirk. He has been married for 34 years to Jessie and has a son, Bruce, and a daughter, Kay. He is also a grandfather of three and a notoriously competitive 12-handicapper at Glenbervie Golf Club.

HUGH WALLACE is the chaplain to Queen's Park Football Club from his base at Mount Florida Church. Born in Glasgow on 30 April 1953, Hugh was educated at Hillhead Primary and Glasgow Academy before going on to Glasgow University for his divinity degree. He served his ministerial probation at Elgin and his first charge was Carluke, before arriving at Mount Florida in 1987. Hugh is married to Rae and has three boys, David, Alasdair and Andrew. They have been to Hampden to see Queen's Park . . . but haven't caught their father's bug as yet.

IAN WILSON was born in Aberdeen in 1958 and joined his home town club as an apprentice at the age of 15. Initially labelled too small to make the grade, Ian has proven everybody resoundingly wrong in a great career that has taken him to Leicester City, Everton and Derby County as well as spells in Turkey and Japan. Capped five times in midfield for Scotland, Ian is now manager of Peterhead and won the BELL'S Third Division Manager of the Year in 2003. He lives in Aberdeen with his wife Tracey, son Greg and daughter Leanne.

WILLIE YOUNG has completed 13 seasons as a Class One referee and has been in charge of over 450 senior matches, including, in recent seasons, four semi-finals in the Scottish Cup and four in the Scottish League Cup as well as the Scottish Cup final between

Hearts and Rangers in May 1998 and has since officiated in 27 countries at 68 European and world matches. Willie was born in Girvan, Ayrshire and educated at Girvan Academy, before going on to Glasgow University to study law where he graduated with a First-Class Honours degree in private law. He is managing partner of one of Scotland's leading legal firms, Brechin Tindal Oatts, and is married to Margot, the principal teacher of home economics at Lochend Community High School in Easterhouse, Glasgow.

1

HOME

GORDON BROWN: I grew up in Fife, part of which I now represent at Westminster, and my earliest football memories are of visits to Stark's Park with my father, a Church of Scotland minister, but a keen supporter of the game. It was New Year's Day, a Raith Rovers v. East Fife match, and I couldn't understand why my father applauded both sets of players. I also sold programmes outside the ground to get in free; my first exercise in finance, and not necessarily high finance. I was standing all the time when selling programmes, and I had to queue up at the beginning of the season to get a slot outside the ground to sell them and you only got in after half-time. I would always be praying that Celtic or Rangers would be playing – to boost the sales.

High finance: Chancellor of the Exchequer Gordon Brown can still sell a mean programme at Stark's Park. (© Photogenix Photography)

ALEX McLEISH: My dad and his best pal took me to my first game at Ibrox. We were at the Govan End, the usual vantage point, where my dad met his pals. Rangers were playing Morton and I can remember it vividly because of the colour of it all. All the games I had seen on television had been in black and white, but even so nothing prepares you for the live event. At that age, around ten, everything seems surreal. It was a beautiful sunny day and both Rangers and Morton had new strips on. Rangers were in blue with red and white socks and Morton had on yellow and blue so I thought: 'This is real theatre.'

STUART COSGROVE: When I was born I was christened Stuart John Francis Cosgrove, so my initials are SJFC, St Johnstone Football Club. I didn't have a lot of choice about whom I supported. Father to son, and occasionally father to daughter, also plays a big part. Proximity has a lot to do with it. When you are a very young child, the roar of the crowd, the lights switched on in mid-winter, and all that stuff, is magical.

TERRY CHRISTIE: I started in football in 1960 when I was in the sixth year at Holy Cross Academy so I have done it non-stop for 43 years and we've only had professional football for 120 years. People joke that I started at the bottom, liked it and stayed there and it's largely true.

DAVID MOYES: I am from Partick originally, and then the family moved to Bearsden. My father was involved with Drumchapel Amateurs, who were one of the biggest in Glasgow in the '60s and '70s. I watched the teams play every Saturday – taken along by my dad – and it no doubt rubbed off on me. Glasgow was a great environment for football with boys playing in the street or in the park, using trees as goalposts. My younger brother played a little bit, and we were brought up as a football family. It was the only sport for me from an early age and it was in-built.

My family gave me everything I ever asked for, but I know, too, my father worked very long hours to make it happen. In Glasgow there was so much of a situation where people went out and ran boys' teams with no money. That working background has been a base for trying to succeed and striving to do better all the time. I joined Celtic as a boys' club player when I was 12 and the people then in the first team were Danny McGrain, who is still the best player I have come across. I was privileged to be in such company.

ALEX McLEISH: I didn't go every week because I was playing myself and didn't get into the fan culture like a lot of my pals. The first boys' club I played for was a club called Rantic and if you dissect that name you can see what it was all about. It had been founded by a guy who wanted an inter-denominational side. It was a good concept and regardless of what primaries or schools we had been to we were in the same boys' club. But funding was difficult and we folded a couple of years later. I went from there to Glasgow United, one of the crack boys' clubs at the time.

I was brought up on street football and of course we never had any of the other distractions like videos and computers. Nowadays the playing areas are few and far between and the kids today don't seem to be getting the same type of exercise we were getting. Whenever I had a spare moment the ball was always out. I was small as a kid and I started primary school life as a striker. I played 11 games and scored 43 goals in my first season in Primary 7. I always had pretty good ball coordination and at that time I had an eye for goal. As I grew up I must have lost all that somewhere along the line!

ALLAN GRIEVE: Before the Second World War the senior team in Stirling were called Kings Park and they played at a ground called Forthbank, which is nowhere near Forthbank, and they were sort of a run-of-the-mill Scottish Second Division side. They never actually got out of the Second Division. They challenged a few times but they never made it and in the summer of 1940 they played the first season of wartime in the sort of Scottish Wartime League. During the summer of 1940 they sustained the only hit from a German bomb anywhere in Stirling. The story is, now you're no' gonna believe this, but it was a German bomber coming back from Clydebank, one of the big raids on Clydebank, and possibly hadn't used all its load and just decided to jettison one of its bombs over any town it passed, and it happened to be Stirling. It also happened to be Kings Park's football ground and it landed slap-bang on top of the grandstand, destroyed the grandstand, and left a great big crater in the pitch, so obviously Kings Park had to stop at that point. For the remainder of the war there was no senior football in Stirling and at the end of the war a group of local businessmen like Tom Ferguson, who'd been involved with Kings Park, decided that it would be better to actually start a new club from scratch. I think there were various reasons for it, Kings Park probably had a few debts and so on that had to be met and I think also if you were a new sports club in 1945 you got extra clothing coupons. So they would get new strips and so on where if it was just the old club reforming they wouldn't have got that so they decided to make the break and Stirling Albion were born. I suppose if there's one person I'd really like to meet it's that German pilot; he's actually responsible for Stirling Albion.

ARTHUR MONTFORD: I have a confession to make: I am a lifelong Morton supporter but I was actually born in Shawlands, Glasgow. But I was brought up in Greenock and my affection for the club started back during the war and the first game I went to was as a small boy in 1940 with the current chairman, Douglas Rae. During the Glasgow blitz Greenock was badly damaged. I was very lucky because I was evacuated to an aunt and uncle in England, two days before they bombed Greenock and I missed it. I was down in England for a couple of years but I always got the local paper sent down to get news of the team to read how they were doing. I did a wee piece on the radio recently and mentioned casually that Stanley Matthews had played for Morton; he actually guested for Morton for a dozen games during the war because he was stationed with the RAF up here. As was Tommy Lawton, so the Morton forward line for a number of games during the war was Stanley Matthews, Tommy Lawton and a young Billy Steel, so that was a sight to see.

ALEX SMITH: I grew up during the war. I was one of seven and my father and older brothers, even the neighbours, took me to football. We stayed in a miners' row and it was a two-room house, nine of us in two rooms with the wash-house and toilets outside. It was tough but everyone mucked in; it was a community. The pit itself policed the village and if anyone stole money in the village they had to get out. If anyone needed bread they got bread. It was a wonderful spirit and if anyone stepped out of line they got sorted out by the pit.

They were people of great principles, unbelievable principles, although some of them were rough diamonds. If you didn't show respect to people your parents got to know about it. Adults were Mr or Mrs.

Jock, Matt Busby, Bob and Bill Shankly and Alex Ferguson, from the shipyards, all came up the same way.

The fantasies you had about football when a kid. I went to see Stirling Albion's first game in the First Division in 1949 and we got beaten 5–1 by Hearts. Willie Bauld scored with a diving header at the top end and I was sitting on the railing by the bottom end and I thought Willie Bauld was level with the top of the crossbar when he met that ball with a horizontal header. Like he was an aeroplane.

Years later I saw a picture of that goal in a programme at Annfield and his two toes were on the turf and he was heading the ball head-high. It was just something in a young boy's mind.

WILLIE McKIE: My father was a farmer and he got a farm in West Fife in 1947. He took me to my first Alloa game in 1948–49 and after that I was hooked. At eight or nine years old I helped Andy Hutton, the trainer, and Tommy Allan, the groundsman, doing odd jobs. I used to run the baths and clean the boots. In 1974 they were looking for a groundsman and I remember George Ormiston interviewing me for the job. I looked after the pitch for 13 years, then I became chief steward and programme editor and in February 1988 I was appointed commercial manager. In the mid-'90s I joined the board, was chairman for two years. I have done just about everything though I can't see them asking me to be manager.

GEORGE ORMISTON: The crowds were quite considerable when I first started, an average of 2,000 to 3,000, and over the years that has diminished. There are too many other diversions these days. In those days there was more of a general interest in football, if there was a cup-tie replay, for example, I would phone all the works in the town, speak to the personnel department and ask if they would let them off work and, sure enough, they did let them off. The town had a big knitting mill, glassworks, seven breweries and pits as well and all these over the years have just disappeared, along with the crowds.

WILLIE McKIE: The bus depot was just next door to the ground, and the double-decker buses sat there with engines running ready for the end of the game. Different times, a different world.

DOUGRAY SCOTT: I was born in Fife and strictly speaking should support Raith Rovers or Dunfermline, but my dad Allan was a big Hibs fan and he took me to see Hibs when I was five. In fact, dad was born in Barrhead in Glasgow but his uncle was a scout for Hibs so he used to go through to Easter Road when he was a boy from Glasgow. I think he sort of toyed with Rangers when he was a kid but quite soon he got into Hibs. I mean, they were a great team in the '50s and you support the team that your dad supports and he used to take me to Easter Road and to home and away games. It wasn't just occasionally, we were quite fanatical about it. We used to go to Arbroath on a Tuesday night and Aberdeen and Inverness; we've been all over Scotland watching Hibs, so we're diehard fans really. Dad played for Queen's Park and I never got to see him play in his prime because he was 50 when I was born, he was playing before the Second World War so that's when he played his football. But he did play in an old crocks' match at Hampden when I was about nine. It was like pre-war against post-war and I watched him playing at Hampden then and that was the first and only time I saw him play football. He could get a membership card so he could take us in and show us round Hampden; I remember doing that quite a few times when I was a boy.

ALEX McLEISH: At Glasgow United we had some really good players and my teammates were training with Celtic and Rangers. There were always scouts about at the games. I was developing slower than the rest; I was a late developer but when I took a stretch round about the age of 16 or 17 I shot up to about 6ft 1in. I moved from centre-forward to midfield and then back to centre-back.

I joined Aberdeen in 1976 when Ally McLeod was in charge, but didn't get my debut until Billy McNeill arrived a year later. Why Aberdeen? My ambition was to play senior professional football and I wasn't going to hang around waiting for one particular club. As I said, I wasn't into fan culture. Rangers were the first result I looked for and it was great they were winning the League and cups, but it wasn't a case of hanging on for them to come and pick me for trials. It was about digging in and being dedicated to my game. I trained with St Mirren for a while, I trained with Hamilton for a while and I would gladly have joined any of those clubs if they had made me the first offer. I never had a game-plan as such – I just wanted to play senior football and I was moving up all the time.

All of a sudden, when I was just about to join Rolls-Royce as an apprentice electrician, having left school with a couple of Highers, I was approached by Bobby Caldwell, the brilliant Aberdeen scout who took a lot of the Glasgow boys up there. My dad and I had a chat with Ally McLeod and dad emphasised that I wanted to continue my studies. So I was working in an accountant's office all day on a Monday and every afternoon after I had done my chores at Pittodrie. It became too much. The first year I did the foundation course then I had to take some more O levels, which were necessary to add to my education portfolio. I was making reasonably good progress with the football club, so much so that they offered me an extension to my contract so it became one or t'other and there was only one winner. I was going to try and be a successful footballer.

PETER DONALD: My interest in football initially was to play the game like most children, but then my father was the manager (in these days he was called the match secretary) of a junior club in Renfrewshire called Johnstone Burgh and Johnstone is my home town so the interest was there from the start. The peak for me was the mid-'60s when Johnstone Burgh were the top junior club and my father was the manager and they all liked me because my dad was involved. The Scottish Junior Cup used to live in my house. One of my mum's neighbours was reminiscing and she was saying how my mother used to have like a museum tour, she had queues of wee boys looking at the cup which used to sit in our living-room and they would chap on my mum's door and ask if they could come in and see the cup. That's really where my interest stems from because my dad was an out-and-out football man.

GORDON BROWN: I have followed Raith Rovers for a long time. There was one great moment in 1995 when they beat Celtic to win the League cup. My flight was delayed from London and I had to listen to it on the telephone. The friend on the other end had a radio and held it to the other end of the phone. I keep saying to people in my speeches when I talk about training and skills that you would be emphasising training and skills, too, if you had to watch Raith Rovers. I think the local teams are worthy of support and in Scotland some of the local teams have not had the support they deserve. I used to watch Aberdeen, and saw Alex Ferguson make his debut for St Johnstone when Charlie Cooke was on the other side.

DOUGRAY SCOTT: I think the first game I saw was Hibs and Celtic when Hibs won 2–1. I was about five and I remember watching it from the South Stand, now called the Famous Five Stand. I have this memory of being a small boy in this massive ground with thousands of people there and I remember it vividly. There was a seated enclosure so I was behind the goals and the advantage of sitting down that end is that the pitch in those days, in fact up until a couple of years ago, sloped, so you saw more of the pitch and you didn't have to be that tall to see it. Other times I was on my dad's shoulders.

I've met Lawrie Reilly a few times and he's great. I played football for my school and various other teams but I never was good enough to even contemplate being a footballer, unfortunately, but I would have loved to have played. I was in the Auchtermuchty High School team and won the cup one year. I played as sweeper, a Franck Sauzee-type role . . . if only. I was quite small for a sweeper but I was quite good at collecting up all the loose balls.

ALLAN GRIEVE: I was actually born in Perth but that was more of an accident. My mother happened to be in Perth when I arrived a month early, to my great regret, that's why I wasn't born in Stirling. But I have been a Stirling Albion supporter from an early age and I always felt that supporting my local team is the thing to do rather than just follow on the bandwagon in supporting one of the big teams. My dad was a football supporter but he actually came from Perthshire and he was really a St Johnstone supporter, but he encouraged me very much to watch the local team and used to come along with me when I was too young to go by myself.

BRIAN FLYNN: I was born in the lucky year of 1957, the year Falkirk last won the Scottish Cup. Forty years later, in '97, we played Kilmarnock in the final again but unfortunately lost this time so I've never seen them win the cup. My mother actually swears that she took me in my pushchair to see the '57 Cup-winning team go through Falkirk with the cup. Now they won the cup in May and I was born in October, so I don't know how she did it. It must have been someone else's baby she had – but she swears it was me.

Mum's not really interested. My dad was a football fan and still is a football fan, and went to see Hibs in the Famous Five years, and went to see Celtic in the time when they won the European Cup and then when I got interested in football he started taking me to see Falkirk. A lot of dads are like that.

BRIAN FLYNN: When the kids come along they take them to see their local team. We stayed only a mile away from the ground and my dad used to drag me down on a Saturday whether I wanted to go or not, it was an excuse for him to go and I remember him taking me to Dunfermline, Kirkcaldy and others and me sitting on the wall outside the pub with a bottle of cola and he was in there having a few pints and I think that was a reason for him to get away on a Saturday from my mother. We used to go in the supporters' bus, and the first game was a Scottish Cup tie at

Brockville and a friend of his gave me a scarf and I thought I was going to the end of the world to see my team go down. It probably was the end of the world actually because we lost 4–1 that day and I was just captivated. Brockville for me was a magical place that you came home from in either floods of tears or tears of joy. I was probably eight or nine or thereabouts. My first memory is of a guy called Sammy Wilson who was an Irish international who played for Falkirk in the late '60s. He shot off-target and it hit me and I remember being doubled up, winded with this thing. It didn't seem to be going very fast or hard but it hit me in the solar plexus and I was carted away by these older guys round about me. That was one of my first memories.

PETER DONALD: In my job as League secretary there have always been these testing west-of-Scotland questions: 'What school did you go to?' and 'who did you support?'. The neutral response for a Glaswegian is to say Queen's Park or Partick Thistle, but I had the response that it was Johnstone Burgh, which no one could take offence at. I played amateur football until I was 38 and it got too sore, a kind of sedentary midfielder. My nickname locally was 'The Tree'; I stood still so long they thought I had taken root. That's the truth. I joined the Scottish Football Association in 1969. It appeared that Chelsea weren't coming to sign me, so I tried to get into football another way and I saw an advert in the *Glasgow Herald*. The SFA were looking for administrative staff. I was training to be a chartered surveyor at the time and do professional exams but I decided that working out how many bricks were in a wall was less exciting than working in football. As secretary of the League I am responsible for all aspects from commercial contracts to generation of fixtures to registration of players to appointment of referees and so on. It really is the nuts and bolts of football. The SFA is a different type of body, much more about education, planning, the national team and all of that. We in the League are competition-driven, so we put on first-team football, reserve football, under-18 football, under-16, league and cup competitions.

CHARLIE REID: When we were growing up during the '70s football was everywhere. It was just part of our lives. My dad was in the army; he played for the Brigade of Guards and before that had signed S-forms with Hibs during the '50s. There's something about family affiliation and first memories, the good memories of going to a game, that stick with you for the rest of your life. If you are like me there is some connection with the people that go before you that goes into supporting a team as well. As a rule of thumb, I also believe you should support the team you were closest to when you were born and when you were growing up.

DAVE MACKAY: I was brought up right by Carricknowe Golf Club and all my father's family were all football people, all Hearts supporters. At six or seven we went to our first match at Tynecastle and would go down early, between 11 and 12 o'clock, for a 3 o'clock kick-off and just sneak under the big iron gate. My dad Tom was a linotype operator, as was my older brother Tommy and my youngest brother Ronnie, and they all worked for the *Scotsman*. Frank, my younger brother, he was an electrician and I was a joiner. I played since I can remember, as just a little kid at Balgreen School, then I went to Saughton School and we finished up winning the cup there. I played left-half and I was a dwarf as a kid. When you saw the photo of the team at Saughton School my brother was at least a foot taller than me and he's only a year older. They went along the line then down to me, the little dwarf, so I had to be a tackler to be able to get into the game. In these days you obviously could tackle from behind but a slide tackle was easy for me, too, because I learned it at a young age.

PETER DONALD: I moved from the SFA to the Scottish

Football League 14 years ago. Jim Farry moved from the SFL to the SFA and I came here as secretary. I actually say it was me plus cash for Farry in the transfer but that's maybe gilding a wee bit. So I came here in 1989, it was the centenary of the Scottish league that year, so they had been in business for 100 years; now it's 114 years. In the time I have been here the biggest single change is probably the commercialisation of the game. Increased money gave it increased opportunities and increased risk, and I think probably the risk has been too great for many. The thing about football is that otherwise sane and sensible men from other areas of life come in and get swept along by the pursuit of glory.

ARTHUR MONTFORD: My one regret of the '40s was that I was doing my national service in Egypt when Morton got to the 1948 Cup final against Rangers. They lost the replay after a 1–1 draw, which as a match still holds the record for people to watch a Cup final; there was 120,000 at the first game and 130,000 at the Wednesday-afternoon replay. Billy Williamson, who didn't play on the Saturday, scored the only goal of the game and the Greenock newspaper reported that the Morton goalkeeper had been blinded by flashlights behind the goal as Williamson scored the winning goal. They were a great side in those days, and they've come and gone a bit since then, but at the moment the great thing about them is that the team is still alive. Two years ago they were 24 hours away from complete liquidation; they were disappearing. I won't go into the legalities or the technicalities, suffice it to say the club was in a perilous state when Douglas Rae stepped in two years ago and saved it. He had to put up money fairly quickly, which he did, and has since spent a lot of money revitalising the ground, giving a good pitch and it all came to fruition on the last day of the season when we had 8,500 for the match which decided the Championship and promotion. I felt very sorry for Peterhead that day because they are a lovely, lovely team, with a nice manager in Ian Wilson, who is a lovely bloke and I was sorry that they missed out. It was a pity that we both couldn't have gone up. A lot of fans stayed loyal to the club. For a while it was 1,500–2,000 during the dark days, being relegated and so on but when we had important matches like our last game against Dundee United, to see who would go into the premier play-off, we got 12,000, and 12,000 in our Cup tie against Celtic. There is a great potential there and it's like most 'provincial' towns, if you can harness some of the fringe Rangers and Celtic support that leave the town every Saturday in buses going to Parkhead and Ibrox, and get a few to support the local club, things would look brighter.

JULIE FLEETING: As a kid I used to play about with my younger brother, Barry – somebody I could kick a ball around with. I lived in Kilwinning when I was growing up, my older cousin lived next door, so me and my brother used to have a kickabout in the street with him and a group of kids in the neighbourhood. When I was nine I joined Cunningham Boys; I was the only girl and at first it was strange. I was actually the only girl in the League and while my team were fine about it some of the other teams that we played against had to get used to it. But after the first game I was just another player in the League. I played in most positions at the boys' club during the three or four years I was there. Dad started taking me to Rugby Park and him, my mum, my brother and sister would watch from the main stand in the seated areas where the families were. I was there for quite a number of years. I have to say I didn't really follow them after my dad left, up until my boyfriend, Colin Stewart, who is a goalkeeper, signed for them and then I would kind of look out for them and see who was involved.

Now that they have released him I'll probably support whoever he goes to.*

---

*Colin is now at Ross County

RICHARD GORDON: I got into football at the age of nine or ten through my dad, who was an Aberdeen fan. My father George died in 1997, but he was the reason I got into football and I still have great memories of him taking me along and going down and sitting over the wall at Pittodrie. Pittodrie was amazing; I still love it now when I see the pictures. There is a lot of footage of the ground and it's great to see what it was like then.

What is now the South Stand was uncovered and was just terracing so we used to get there as early as possible and I used to get down the front, with legs over the wall. The memory as much as anything and the thing that sticks with me is the midweek matches and the excitement of being there and seeing these giants, as they were to me, in the red strip. It was a magical experience.

CHARLIE REID: My dad was a joiner and work took him, and us, down to Cornwall and then to Fife. He worked on building sites in England and my mum was a district nurse down there. I think they got a bit homesick and they moved back at the end of 1972. Dad was a Hibs man, but one of those Edinburgh guys who also went to Tynecastle. I remember talking to Jimmy Reid, who was born in Glasgow, and he told me he regularly went and watched Hibs just because they had a great side.

The first Hibs game I saw was when I was nine or ten years old and they won 7–1. The next weekend we came back up from Cornwall and Dad took me to Tynecastle and we saw Hearts beat Falkirk 1–0. But it was no contest – everything about Hibs appealed to me; maybe it was the strip or something. Young kids quite often have odd reasons for taking up a team. The fact is Hibs also played really good football and were by far the better side in Edinburgh at the time. First impressions count and for that first game, Dad took us into the stand and just walking up and sitting down and seeing what was in those days probably the biggest terracing in Scotland outside Hampden made a massive impression. The fact that they scored so many goals and their football was absolutely magical had a lifelong impact. Even when the teams have been utterly appalling my feelings have never changed.

After our first TV appearance on *The Tube* in 1987, we moved back to Edinburgh from Auchtermuchty because we had no car and we wanted to get into the pubs and clubs to play. We literally didn't have any money and between leaving Fife and getting signed for a record deal we were on the dole most of the time, so we went to football only when we could afford it – maybe 12 home games a season at most.

RICHARD GORDON: The big thing when I started going to Pittodrie was going to whichever end Aberdeen were shooting at for the first half and at half-time, heading for the other end. If there was a big away support, they just started to make their way round to the other half, and we'd all pass and we never had any problems. There was a magic about it, just because you were wee and the stadiums all seemed so big. Nowadays I understand the reasons for all-seaters, and I'm of an age now where I probably prefer the comfort, but I still miss that and quite often when I'm at games I will still stand to watch the game rather than sit down. To me a lot of these stadiums are soulless places: McDiarmid Park, Firhill, Old Trafford. They are like identikit stadiums and they could be anywhere in the country and it's going to take a long time before those stadiums build up their own history.

JULIE FLEETING: The crowd at Rugby Park were always noisy, they always got a huge support even though they were in the Second Division and I always remember them singing from the terracing. It was always a good atmosphere – we loved going to the game. The year they got promoted to the First Division there was a pitch invasion after the game. My uncle lifted us down off the stand on to the park to join in.

I just loved playing much more than watching; it was always just great fun. After the boys' club I moved to Prestwick Girls, who later became Ayr United, and I was with them for eight years. They were very, very well organised. They had been running for quite a few years, and were one of the biggest girls' teams in Scotland and I made a lot of very good friends there. At the time I didn't realise it would be possible to make a career out of it which is why I focused a lot on my education, at Edinburgh University.

ALLAN GRIEVE: Mother was just a kind of long-suffering person who put up with non-stop football talk. My first visit to see my home team came when I was about three years old, and I don't remember a great deal about it other than it was at the start of the season, and it was baking hot at Stirling Albion's old ground Annfield. I was more interested in the swarms of wasps that seemed to be going about. Annfield was well known for swarms of wasps and I think when they built the terracing they had originally just used banking of any old rubbish they could get and they didn't put a sort of skin of concrete on it and the concrete was all cracked and there were holes and gaps in it, a sort of perfect breeding ground under there for all sorts.

Of my early memories back in the early 1960s that is certainly one of them. Also from that time memories of Stirling Albion playing in the old First Division competing at the highest level with the likes of Celtic and Rangers and so on and actually, in fact, drawing with Celtic at Annfield the year Celtic won the European Cup, 1967.

RICHARD GORDON: At Brockville in 1970 I sat there as a boy and looked around the old stand, the dirty glass and barbed wire. When I went back there in 1990 I was working for Radio Clyde and doing a report on a match for them and I walked in and nothing had changed. It was like stepping back in time almost 20 years and it just brought the whole day flooding back. I think that's what they mean about being bitten early – it just becomes like an obsession. Every week we would go down and stand outside from midday onwards and we would get the same autographs every week, from the players – who were like gods – as they came in. I never stepped inside the hidden depths at Pittodrie until I was in the media, all those years later. I remember once or twice players going down for training sessions in the summer at Westburn Park and in that sense they were out and about but they were the town's team and most of my friends supported them, the local boys. There didn't seem to be the same proliferation of Old Firm fans about in Aberdeen then as there certainly are now. As a kid my uncle stayed near Bobby Clark, the goalkeeper, and arranged for me to meet him. I was ten years old at the time, so I was down at my uncle's house and he took me round to Bobby's and Bobby drove up in this MG Midget and got out, and I said, 'Hello, Mr Clark,' and he took me into his house, got a photograph and signed it for me. I played in goals at the time, so he was my hero.

LAWRIE REILLY: I was born very close to the Hearts ground actually, within half a mile, but I was brought up a Hibs supporter because my dad and his parents and brothers were all Hibs fans. My father worked on the railway so we travelled free and I was in every football ground in Scotland before I was ten, following the Hibs. My dad was a guard, so we all travelled in the guard's van. I played at Merchiston Primary and then I went to Boroughmuir, a rugby-playing school. I didn't mind it, but football was my game and you had only one of everything – a pair of pants, a pair of boots.

Bobby Clark.
(© *Aberdeen Press and Journal*)

Lawrie Reilly (front row, second from right) in his school team
(photo courtesy of Lawrie Reilly).

So if you played football in the morning you couldn't play rugby in the afternoon. I went to all the matches at Easter Road with my dad, but I used to nip down and see the Hearts occasionally because they opened the gates 20 minutes before the finish and you could nip in or ask somebody to lift you over the turnstiles. I supported every team that played against the Hearts.

RICHARD GORDON: In the professional sense it's been fantastic, obviously, as time has moved on and Aberdeen had a hugely successful time during the '80s. I started working at Northsound in 1987 when it was beginning to tail off. I missed Fergie by about six months; by that stage Ian Porterfield had taken over and that was just awful because it all began to fall apart very, very quickly. But then Alex Smith and Jocky Scott stabilised the club and Aberdeen won the two cups in 1989 and '90, and very nearly won the League in 1991. That was another heartbreaking situation. I was actually down in Glasgow by then but I did the commentary for Northsound Radio and in those days you could only do the last five minutes of the first half, so for the first 40 minutes I'm just sitting in the box watching the game. Then whoever is in the studio hands over to me and I start: 'Good afternoon, welcome to Ibrox Stadium . . . and Rangers have had their chances and Aberdeen are holding on' – at which point Mark Walters whipped a cross in and Mark Hateley scored and that was it. We had been on air for about 20 seconds and you knew the league title was heading to Ibrox. That was a really hard one to deal with that day.

BRIAN FLYNN: I was never any good at football – a double-decker bus could turn quicker than me – but I loved watching it. I always say I'm not a football fan, I'm a Falkirk supporter. You know people who say, 'I used to follow so-and-so but I'm now a Manchester United fan', I mean, you're either a man or a woman, a Falkirk fan or not a Falkirk fan. A mate of mine is a Stoke City fan but he goes to see Man United as well, so what's all that about? If you're a Stoke fan you should go and see Stoke every week, home and away. I missed two games last season, but only because it was just impossible to get there. From a business point of view, the pub has also a good relationship with East Stirling, Stenhousemuir and Stirling Albion as well.

ALLAN GRIEVE: Annfield was unique. It was built in a big estate quite close to the centre of Stirling, but it was almost like being in a rural environment. There were trees around the ground, big old trees. It was a very open ground, and you could change ends at half-time and so on. There was no segregation in those days and Albion fans always used to congregate behind the goal that Albion were shooting into. It was a ritual to change ends at half-time, although when we were in the First Division, standing at that end, we didn't usually see very much in the way of action, it was all mostly at the other end. Off the top of my head George Peebles scored for Albion against Celtic that day. He was a

Stirling man, a Stirling guy who had played for Dunfermline for many years at a high level. He played in Europe for them, and then finished his playing days at Stirling then became a coach and eventually became manager of the club in the late 1980s.

RICHARD GORDON: I left school in 1977 and worked for Clydesdale Bank for ten years. It was a job, it was secure, I was earning half-decent money at the time and I moved up the ladder, but strangely enough never saw myself as a bank manager. But I was a huge football fan throughout and towards the end of that time I met a guy, an old pal called Alan Thompson, who worked in the merchant navy and I hadn't seen him for years and we had a couple of pints and went to a midweek Aberdeen game. As we were watching the game Alan said: 'I normally sit over there in the main stand. I'm working for hospital radio these days. It's great fun and you get to pretend that you're on the real radio.' Anyway I went up to the hospital radio studio with Alan and it was great. It was run on a shoestring but the first day I was up there it was a Saturday afternoon and they were just starting off the sports programme and the guy who was hosting it just turned to me and asked if I wanted to come in. I had never done anything like that before, but we were just going to be talking about football, so I sat there and talked about it and the bug bit, the way that football had 17 or 18 years earlier. I started doing the sports programme and some reporting and commentary, along with other bits and bobs just to get the experience of sitting down in front of a microphone. From there I wrote to Ken McRobb at Northsound – their football programme had been off the air and they were coming back just at the start of 1987 – who was in charge at the time and just said if you need anybody then I've got a bit of experience from hospital radio. I'm great, hire me! He actually phoned me on Hogmanay, late afternoon/early evening to offer me the chance to be a part-time reporter – I started covering the Dons games for them part-time – and then three or four months later he offered me the job as trainee journalist which was a great chance. I obviously had to weigh it up: the steady secure career in the bank and a cheap mortgage or an offer which at the time was six grand a year less. I grabbed it with both hands.

LAWRIE REILLY: I can remember Mitchell Downie played in goal and Ginger Watson played left-back for Hibs. Once, in the station at Stirling – we had travelled to see them – all the players came along and I went up to one with red hair. I was only about eight or nine and I said: 'Hello, Ginger,' and he said, 'The name's Mr Watson to you.' My dad was absolutely raging that you could treat a wee laddie like that. During the war a lot of kids were evacuated although I think there was only one bomb dropped on Edinburgh. I'm sure they were aiming at Tynecastle!

RICHARD GORDON: It was a really steep learning curve. Kenny left within a few weeks and another presenter left and very quickly I was presenting six or seven shows a week – news, music, sport – and working about 75 hours a week. But it was a young team there and we were all really enthusiastic. We covered things like the Piper Alpha disaster, the Chinook helicopter crash in the Mull of Kintyre; there were lots of big, big stories up there at the time, so we all just learned the job on the run and it stood me in good stead. Three years later I went down to Radio Clyde and came out of sport. It lasted 14 or 15 months and then I applied for a job with the BBC in Glasgow. The last four or five years it has been the presentation bit, a bit of telly and in the main the radio because it's what I love and there is no bigger buzz. I still get the thrill every time I go on air, and the buzz of being on live for three, four, five hours, whatever it is, and really not knowing where the programme is going. You know the game is kicking off at such and such a time but you just never know what is around the corner. The buzz is of being live and flying by the seat of your pants.

TERRY CHRISTIE: My mother was from a very sporting family and we lived at a place called Craigentinny in one of the housing schemes which is a ten-minute walk from Easter Road, so on a Saturday just after the war just about every adult male went to the match. It was a five-day week, and they worked until lunch time on Saturday, got changed and went to the match. It was like the lemmings. Just about every adult went to watch the Hibs and there were hordes from miles away. It was a hard time, the rationing was still on the go and the pubs shut at 10 p.m. and 3 p.m. on a Saturday. There was a hunger for football and Hibs provided entertainment with the Famous Five. I grew up thinking nobody could play football like Hibs and the Famous Five – they were wonderful players. Gordon Smith was the best, but Lawrie Reilly was poaching goals and Bobby Johnston had skill that you can't believe. Willie Ormond, who made his home in Musselburgh – all his grandchildren came to my school – was the workhorse in the team. But he had this wonderful shot and never missed a penalty kick. Hibs were a huge thing in our lives and then the team fell away a bit.

Hibs and Rangers line up before a five-a-side match at Tynecastle in 1949. Left to right: Willie Waddell, Jock Weir, Alex Venters, Bobby Baxter, Willie Finnegan, Dr Adam Little, Willie Woodburn, Lawrie Reilly, Charlie Watkins, Gordon Smith. It was Lawrie Reilly's first game in a Hibs jersey.
(© The Scotsman Publications Limited)

ALLAN GRIEVE: Over the years Stirling Albion have had their fair share of winning the lower divisions. I mean we were known as the yo-yo team in the '50s and '60s because we went up one year and down the next; you know, we've won more Second Division Championships and so on than most clubs. In my time supporting them, we've won three Second Division Championships, in 1977, 1991 and 1996. Stirling, I'm afraid, is not really a football town. However well we do we struggle to attract big crowds. Even when we were winning the Second Division out of sight in 1996, we were doing very well to attract 1,000 of our own fans to the games. Part of the reason for that is I think Stirling has a lot of incomers to it. A lot of the big employers in Stirling like the University and Scottish Amicable – Prudential as it is now – have drawn people into the area, but they're not Stirling through and through. Like a lot of teams we suffer through being that bit too close to Glasgow and people are brought up to support one or other of the Glasgow sides, so the town doesn't recognise or get behind the club like it could do.

DAVE MACKAY: In the school holidays, on the Monday, you went up Saughton Park, which had at least ten pitches and our street, or our area, used to go up there and take on other streets or other areas. You always had your sandwiches and your bottle of water. You only played 15 or 20 minutes then went off.

TERRY CHRISTIE: Another thing about those days is that there were no floodlights, so if you had Cup replays they had to be afternoon kick-offs – and at school I was a clever wee boy, a wee swot. But if there was a Cup replay away, I was allowed to play truant. My mother would give me a note to get off at lunchtime and get up and get either the tram or the bus up to the station and away on the football special. So although all her hopes and dreams were set on this wee clever laddie she had, I was allowed to truant school to watch the Hibs.

DAVE MACKAY: I was a ball player anyway. People tended to think that, even when I went to Tottenham with Danny Blanchflower. The attitude was that Danny's a footballer and Davie Mackay's the hard man, and some people didn't consider me a footballer. That was rubbish. I actually never lost in a Cup final, maybe 30 or 40 in all, going back to my school days. At Saughton School Mr Newland and Mr Moyes were the two teachers who ran the football and they never entered for the Scottish Cup. The whole of Scotland did, but they didn't think we would have a chance. The following year they put us in and we won, so I think if they had put us in a year earlier we must have had a chance. We drew 0–0 with King's Park, at Hampden, and beat them 2–1 at our beloved Tynecastle and my brother Tommy scored the winning goal.

STUART COSGROVE: I went to my first games at five or six. At that time St Johnstone had a ground called Muirton Park, a traditional Scottish working-class ground on the fringes of a housing scheme called Muirton and that was where I fell in love with the Saints and the team of the late '50s that I first saw as a kid and whose names I can recite to this day. Billy Taylor, the goalkeeper, works at Luton Airport in their security division and when I go through Luton I always look out for him. Now they wouldn't be in my Top 10 Saints teams of all time but because they were the first there is always that nostalgia. My father died when I was seven. He drove a Co-op Dairy lorry and drove me down to Queen of the South with Saints flags on the windows and the mirrors. It was the farthest you could go; two miles down the road it was England. When he died it was quite traumatic but my uncle Billy, my father's brother and the main adult in my life, thought he would look after me and one of the first things he did was redecorate my bedroom. He said to me: 'In 20 years' time someone will scrape off this wallpaper and what we have to do is to paint every wall with St Johnstone teams.' So behind the wallpaper we had all the teams from that era, all the players set out in formation.

DAVE MACKAY: When I played at Hearts it was 11 against 11. The outside-left was marked by the right full-back; it was easy then but when they started to change it got a bit complicated. I went out there and if it's 50–50 then I'm going to win it, not by going over the ball or anything. I wanted to win at anything, five-a-side, darts, anything.

STUART COSGROVE: My house in Leatham, the biggest housing scheme in Perth, was on a hill and you could see the whole of Perth almost. From the upstairs windows I could see Muirton Park and before I went to bed I could look at the park. Curiously, when they left the ground and did a deal with Asda and moved to McDiarmid Park, I could look out the window and see McDiarmid Park, so that must be only one of two or three houses in Perth where you can see both grounds. When you were a kid you would go and pick berries or tatties, that was how you earned your money, and McDiarmid's and a load of other farms in that area was where we picked tatties. The original house I was born in, Primrose Crescent in Tulloch – another housing scheme in Perth – is actually the back gardens of McDiarmid Park, so I was literally born into it.

There's a kid now in the team who I think will be the next big one we will sell on, Mark Baxter, and he lives in that street in Tulloch as well. Sandy McLaren, the former Scottish goalkeeper, was also born there.

LAWRIE REILLY: After school I went to a team called Murrayfield Athletic and I played inside-forward for them and then I was asked to go to Edinburgh Thistle, who trained at Easter Road. We trained at one side of the field and the Hibs trained at the other and you used to spend your time seeing if you knew any of the big names that were training. A very successful team, Edinburgh Thistle. We won the Scottish Juvenile Cup; we won seven cups in the 1944–45 season and only lost one game, our 50th, when one of the lads didn't turn up. Hearts wanted me. The manager sent word to my house asking if I would come down to Tynecastle to have a word with him and my dad said 'that's fine' and then went and told Hibs. So I signed for the Hibs at 16 and a month and when I was 17 they gave me £20 for signing on, and put £2 in the bank account for me every week. Gordon got £10 for signing on and I always kid him on that I must have been twice as good as him.

CRAIG LEVEIN: My two brothers first got me interested in football and every night after school it was down the local park in Aberdour, kicking the ball till it was dark and we had to go in. I just had an interest for as long as I can remember. Initially I supported Raith Rovers because my uncle took me to Stark's Park on a regular basis when I was ten or eleven years old. The very first match I remember being at was actually a Motherwell v. Rangers game when I was five or six because my other uncle supported Motherwell!

At that age I didn't see much, to be honest, because it was all terracing, but by the time I was 14 I was going by myself with some of my pals. A couple of seasons later we were going home and away to every game. When I first went to Stark's, Murray McDermott, who died recently, was in goal and Donald Urquhart and Bertie Miller are other names I remember. Billy Brown, who was assistant manager here recently, he was in a lot of the early games I watched. The crowds were massive. One of the seasons I watched them they had the chance of going up from the Second Division to the first – we followed them that season – and we went to watch matches at Stirling Albion, the third- or fourth-last games of the season, and then up to Dundee for the last or second-last game. I remember that being quite an exciting year and the season after that I was playing for a junior club, Lochore Welfare. I played at Lochore for a season and a half; and you grow up quickly at 16 or 17 when you're playing with some real men, so I learned what you could get away with and what you couldn't get away with. You learned just how tough you were and it was no place for the faint-hearted. I remember playing up at Thornton one night. This guy had the ball at his feet inside the penalty box, with his back to the goal, so I poked my leg through between his legs, knocked the ball away and ran round the other side and cleared it. As I'm watching the ball going up the other end of the park with everybody else, next thing I'm flat on the deck. You had to be streetwise and be aware of what was going on round about you. I certainly stayed away from him for the rest of the night. But that was good grounding for me. I signed for Cowdenbeath in 1981 when Andy Rolland was manager and it was obviously more professional at the league grounds – bigger crowds with better players. Andy was a really decent guy, but the learning came through the experience itself, playing against slightly better players. Before I moved to Hearts we played them in a League Cup tie. We drew at Cowdenbeath and we drew at Tynecastle then we got beaten on penalties. It was that experience of being able to play better teams in the League and in Cup ties as well.

JULIE FLEETING: The American thing came out of the blue. I think San Diego Spirit had seen a tape of me playing and decided to offer me a contract. They still had a space on the roster for a foreign player and luckily for me it was right after I was graduating so it came along at a perfect time.

CRAIG LEVEIN: My mum told me that from the age of five or six all I said was that I wanted to be a professional footballer. I certainly worked hard at it. I spent a lot of time practising by myself and working hard physically and trying to progress. I was doing a lot of fitness stuff; in the house I used to do sit-ups and press-ups on a nightly basis, because at that age everything helps. I was desperate to get a chance to play at a high level and once I played a while at Cowdenbeath, I realised I could play at that level and I was definitely determined to move up.

TERRY CHRISTIE: Oh, Dundee destroyed teams, they just destroyed teams. Billy Steel was very much a right-half, but he sat in midfield, protected his centre-half and was solid in possession, and a great passer of the ball. Bobby Wishart could get forward as well and he scored a lot of goals because if Bobby was in the box he generally scored. Bobby Cox was captain of the club, and they later named a stand after him. It was all young guys getting on well together.

LAWRIE REILLY: Of the Famous Five, I was the second to sign for Hibs, although I was the second youngest. Eddie Turnbull

came out of the Navy and signed and Willie Ormond was transferred from Stenhousemuir and they went straight into the first team. Then wee Bobby Johnston, he was the last one to come in to make up the five. I feel sorry for a lot of these guys who were very good footballers but spent a lot of their best years, their best soccer years, in the forces. I had been playing outside-left, but Scotland put me centre-forward with Jimmy Mason and then back on the left with Billy Steel. Wee Steely had been in the forces too and he was a veteran compared with me. He liked a cigarette, wee Billy loved to smoke,

Billy Whizz: Billy Steel was Scotland's wing star.
(© *Daily Record*/Mirrorpix)

always had a fag, but I think it used to catch up with him – the breathing, you know – so accidentally I moved inside and he went on the wing and he stayed on the wing and I ran about, because I was naturally an inside player. The Famous Five, as they call us; I always felt the famous six at the back didn't get the credit they deserved. I mean, you had to stop teams scoring as well and we had a lot of good players that played at the back.

CRAIG LEVEIN: It was while we were actually playing Hearts that Sandy Jardine spoke to me and told me that Hearts were interested. It was something that appealed to me; it wasn't far away from home as I was living in Dunfermline at that time and I thought it was a great oportunity. The manager at the time was Alex McDonald and they had a good team: Sandy Jardine, Willie Johnston, Jimmy Bowen, Roddy McDonald, Stewart McLaren, George Cowie, Danny McKay, John Robertson, Davie Bowman and Donald Park were there at the time. I joined in the December of 1983, and they had a European qualification place in that 1983–84 season. It was great when I stepped into a team that was going quite well and I thoroughly enjoyed it, despite the injuries. My first injury was in 1986 and I was out for over a year. I came back, played for two or three months and then I was out for another year and didn't get back playing on a consistent basis till the end of the '89 season. It was my cruciate ligaments, and that happened twice. At that time the surgery wasn't quite as pioneering as it is now, as recovery periods were a year rather than the six months or less that they take just now, so it was quite a new operation at the time. From '89 I played till 1995 when I re-injured the same kneecap and that was me finished, although I didn't know it at the time. The last game I played I would be 31 years old. I tried another few operations and it didn't work, and I finally gave up, and left the club in 1997. First of all I left to go and coach at Livingston for four or five months with Jim Leishman (unpaid, I may add, and he still owes me money!), then I joined Cowdenbeath as manager in December 1997.

LAWRIE REILLY: There was never animosity, you know. There was one day we had played well and photographers came into the dressing-room after the game and they wanted a photograph of the five of us and Jock Govan said: 'Jesus Christ, there's the team getting their photograph taken again.' There was a lot of good banter and of course the Famous Six were getting bonuses. We were winning and they were reaping the benefit of us winning.

JACK McCONNELL: Like everyone else I kicked a ball around from an early age and there was a great local village league in Arran – hard, competitive stuff with a lot of farmers in the team, and quite rough. You can imagine how competitive it can get on an island. I was never quite tall enough or fast enough to play in midfield or up front so I played left-back. I used to want to make sure the opposition knew I was on the pitch. That made up for what I lacked in speed.

LAWRIE REILLY: It was a newspaper started the Famous Five thing. It just happened to stick, the same as Last-Minute Reilly. It was a newspaper that wrote that when we drew at Wembley: 'Last-Minute Reilly saves the day' or something like that; it's always 'Last-Minute Reilly'. They forget I've got a nice name, Lawrence. My first game for Hibs was at Kilmarnock. I was only 16 at the time and they played me inside-right to Gordon Smith, which was just a dream come true. We won 4–3, and I didn't score any goals or anything. In fact, I don't know how I played because every time I got the ball I was always looking for Gordon to pass it to, even if somebody might have been in a better position.

STUART COSGROVE: Memories tend to merge into a season rather than a single game. You could move round the ground from one end to another. I have programmes going back to those days, and photographs of the '50s teams framed and hanging in my kitchen. I can picture being there.

The most profound memory was the walk to the ground, because as you came down through the scheme you had to walk down this really long railway path and then over a footbridge and then you were at the ground. This cinder path seemed to go on forever. That bridge was actually the marshalling yards and that was where the goods trains were and it was 24 hours a day when they were changing trains and I can vividly remember the clanking and the floodlights which were probably as strong, if not stronger, than the Saints lights, which they had bought from Arsenal. So looking out my window at night it always seemed there were floodlights on.

JOHN HUGHES: When people say to me you're from Edinburgh, I like to tell them I'm a Leither – most Leithers know what I mean. My dad was a docker all his days and I come from a family of two brothers, three sisters, and my mother came up with a family of twelve, all brought up in a single end. I love Leith, I love the environment, I love the people. I just feel Leith people are special, they've got that sense of humour, that wicked sense of humour and you get to know the people and I can walk out the door and it's a toot o' the horn or a nod o' the head and it's a wave or a wink and 'How you doin?' If I went from here down into the Kirkgate Shopping Centre it would take me 45 minutes to get there, stopping and talking and 'How are you doin?' Everybody wants to know and you feel that everybody really wants you to do well. Ian McCall winds me up all the time because he knows how much it means to me and he says that the postcode for Leith is EH6. Now I'm just up at Restalrig, he says, 'I hear your postcode has changed to EH7', and I say, it's still EH6, it's still the Leith postcode. I've got Leith in my blood.

When we were young we were out in the street playing

football, kicking the ball against windows and doors and everything like that and I always got told to go down the public park and play but that seemed too much of a hassle for us, too organised for us. So you painted the goalposts on the wall and away you went.

My father was a great sportsman who played junior football and his claim to fame was he never got sent off and he keeps reminding me of that. He says, 'I don't know where you come frae, you must have got it frae your mother's side,' although she never played football. He's my hero, you know.

He's in ill health at the moment, he's had a couple of strokes and he's lost his speech but he sticks his fingers up at you, gives you the thumbs-up. He's a gentleman.

DAVID MOYES: At Parkhead part of the job was cleaning the terraces to get ready for a game on Saturday and I honestly never thought anything of it. Obviously we would rather have been playing football, but we saw that as really just a chance to be inside the stadium with the lights on. A lot of people outside would have given their right arms just to be cleaning the terraces at Parkhead. I was still at school, and only coming in a couple of nights a week, but accepting that if Celtic wanted it done we would do it.

Frank Connor ran the S-forms – another great character. Jimmy Lumsden, who works with me here now, he was there and guys like this would have a full day at Celtic Park till six at night then take the S-forms till eight or nine at night. That is a typical working football man in Glasgow. He never looked at his watch; if the players were there he would be there.

I became full-time at 16, got in the first team and had a great period to start. But then the manager changed and when Davie Hay took over things changed for me. But I was fortunate enough to be brought up in the company of a team full of international players and I still believe that what I learned in those few years is with me now. They had a fantastic period where they didn't lose any games whether it was first team, youth or reserves and it was something built in the club. They were also a club renowned for attacking football and I like my teams to be that way – something the public can enjoy.

LAWRIE REILLY: For training they used to have you on road runs, round Arthur's Seat with the trainer following on a bike. It was great, we were a winning team and the camaraderie was fabulous. There were always pranks getting played on folk, jokes, and it was a great atmosphere. You were looking forward to going training, you couldn't get there quickly enough.

DAVID McGREGOR: Football is still the main sport in Angus, but like a lot of places it's not as big a football region as it was at one time. In my youth, the late '50s, early '60s, apart from Forfar there were three junior teams, about six amateur teams playing on a Saturday. Nowadays there's ourselves, two junior teams and one amateur team.

My father, also David, has been a season ticket holder since the early '60s. My boyhood hero as a Forfar player was Donald McKay who subsequently went on to manage Blackburn Rovers. Donald was our goalkeeper and he was a youngster from Perth at the time setting out on a lengthy football career. The first game I can really remember was in 1958 when we got beat 9–1 by Rangers. There was a crowd of 9,000 for a Scottish Cup game and Forfar played them a year later at Station Park and they only beat us 3–1 that time. But we had reasonable results against Rangers. In season 1976–78, in the semi-final of the League Cup we were 2–1 up with seven minutes to go at Hampden then lost 5–2 in extra-time. We drew 0–0 in the 1982 Scottish Cup semi-final, then lost the replay 3–1 having been reduced to ten men after only half an hour. Then we also played them in a League Cup tie in '85. At the time we were redeveloping one side of our ground and we were drawn at home and we had to play the game at Dens Park then we lost in a penalty shoot-out after drawing 2–2 after extra-time. Ian McPhee, one of Forfar's greatest players, had a chance to win it in the penalty shoot-out and missed and we lost it. My father and mother always bought me a season ticket and we used to stand just behind the bottom goal never thinking I would end up being chairman some day.

JOHN HUGHES: Dad was a Celtic supporter, because his family are Irish. He was brought up in Lochend and when he met my mother their first house was a room and kitchen in the Kirkgate. They moved back there in 1964, the year I was born, and I got lost in the flitting for a couple of hours and had to be picked up by a neighbour. My father's still in the same house. He's a typical docker. He liked a drink, a couple of pints, and he liked to work. He always worked, he was never idle. We call him old Don Corleone, because he's like the Godfather to us. My brother's got a pub, The Ferret and Bootlace, and we get him in. He's on the zimmer and everybody looks after him and makes sure that he's looked after and he just sits in the corner and watches what's going on and he drinks his half pint and his dark rum and it's great. I saw him later on eventually when he played for Leith Dockers and we used to go along on a Sunday and watch him. He was older then, he played centre-half. He was only about 5 ft 11 in., maybe a bit taller, but his timing in the air was impeccable. I noticed from an early age the way he read the game and all that and passed the ball and you could tell he played the game in a great manner.

LORD MACFARLANE: We lived in the West End of Glasgow and so, like most people who lived there, my father was a Partick Thistle supporter and like most young boys at that time I was lifted over the turnstiles for many, many years. The Partick Thistle interest never, as most Thistle supporters know, leaves them. No matter what they do, who they play for, what other teams they support, they always have an interest in Thistle.

I was always interested during school, but I went to a rugby-playing school and so I played rugby until my last years at school when I played at Hampden for Queen's Park. There were four teams at that time, the Victoria XI and the Hampden XI, The Strollers and the first team and I was playing rugby for the school in the morning and football in the afternoon for the Hampden XI or the Strollers until the chap who ran the Strollers pointed out that I might play better in the afternoon if I didn't play rugby in the morning.

JOHN HUGHES: As kids we all had a crewcut, you know, and there used to be pots because she couldn't afford to do individual meals and things like that because it was that big a family. It used to be big pots on the go, either mince and tatties, stovies, tripe or homemade soup and if you weren't eating the stovies anything that was left went into the pot and that would be on the go. That's what I say to everybody when they're all eating pasta: I got brought up on tripe and stovies and ma ma's homemade soup. Even now when I taste a bowl of soup I say, 'It's no' like ma ma's' – she just had a knack. If there was tripe on the go if you weren't in quick you missed out because aunties, uncles, cousins, they were all in for it. I still love it to this day but nobody can do it like ma mother, you know, and it was brilliant. My mum's house was like a gang hut, honestly like a gang hut, and it was everybody for themselves. You didn't make a cup of tea in my mother's house because if you made one you had to make two pots of tea there were that many people in visiting. My mother, she held the whole family together.

LAWRIE REILLY: I stopped playing in 1957. I got an injury against Ireland years before – a bang on the knee – and it was never right. Then I got cartilage problems and had the operation and the surgeon said to me, 'You've a lot of arthritis in your knee, you'll have problems with that,' and he's been right enough, I've had arthritis problems ever since. The newspapers came and asked me if would join them. I had bought a pub a year before called The Bowler's Rest in Leith and a lot of supporters used to come. What I liked was when the Rangers played the Hibs at Easter Road there was a section of the Rangers Supporters' Club, their bus came right to my pub, and they all came in and we never ever had any trouble whatsoever. In these days a lot of footballers had pubs: me, Gordon, Jock Govan, Eddie Turnbull, Willie Ormond. Like my mother and father I never drank in my life and I've never found it a problem running a pub and not drinking, although some people found it odd.

JOHN HUGHES: We all used to go up to Easter Road. We'd sneak in or it would be the lift-overs. In those days, you know, you got a lift over or you could climb the wall or get a chuckie over the wall.

In the 1970s at Hibs it was your Pat Stantons and all that and the first game that really stuck in my head was a European game that they won 6–1, and Jim O'Rourke scored a hat-trick. I was a Hibs supporter, always supported Hibs, but when I got a bit older I started jumping about with a couple of boys who supported Celtic and they used to go in the Leith Supporters bus through to Parkhead, but Hibs were always my team.

I was fortunate enough to train with Hibs when I was in there as a schoolkid, two nights a week, when I was about 14 or 15.

A lot of folk don't know that I signed for Arbroath when I was 16. Three of us went and the manager was a boy called Ian Stewart. I got on the fringes of the first team but fortunately at the end of that year he gave me a free transfer so that allowed me to come back and go and play with all my mates.

FRANK McAVEETY: I was brought up in Springburn in north-east Glasgow, an area which had a lot of railway works. We were just like any other ordinary working-class family, obsessed with playing football in the back courts, and my experience as a youngster was just chalking the back wall of a tenement. Our house was where the big Woolworths store was which had a major wall on it so you just chalked out the goalposts and you played between. I had two older brothers, one four years older and one two years older, and a brother who was four years younger, and we all played football. When we moved to what was considered a sort of 'desirable' house – a five-apartment with a big side garden and a back garden – within 24 hours, because of the Irish genes in our family instead of it being a football pitch it was turned over for a plot of land for potatoes and carrots. This was the year Labour lost the General Election, 1970. There was one good bit and one bad bit in that year because England also lost in the World Cup – to the greatest football side I've ever seen. Moving was a magical experience because you had the big garden, you had the inside toilets and you had the space to do things. My dad was a general labourer, a butcher, van salesman and then in the late '60s he was a cleansing van driver and then a post office sorting man and then, latterly, a security guard in hospitals. My dad was unskilled. My father fell out with Celtic when they sold Paddy Crerand to Manchester United. Dad was born in the Gorbals and his family was from Donegal, and he refused for years to go back. He gave up running the supporters' bus in disgust over that. He took me to the Cup finals but he wasn't an 'every week' guy because he was so disgusted that Celtic sold his hero. They sold Bertie Auld, too. Any more and I'll be greetin'!

JOHN HUGHES: In the juniors with Newtongrange Star I was playing against older people and I remember one game in the Scottish Cup, it was 0–0 with a minute to go and I was getting really frustrated. I hit this older guy with a tackle, a real heavy tackle, and he didn't say too much. The referee blew the whistle and split us up and as I shook his hand going off the park, he said, 'Oh, young yin, I'll see you next week.'

I said, 'Aye, nae problem, I'm ready for you.'

Ten minutes into the replay: 'smack', broken ankle. That's how you learn your lesson. It was a great grounding for me, really toughened me up. While I was in the juniors I got a chance to go to East Fife, who were top of the Second Division, or Berwick Rangers, who were bottom of the First Division. East Fife were offering better money, but Jimmy Thomson was the manager at Berwick and he was a docker beside my father, so I went there. I picked up an injury in the first game of the season so I was off for about four or five months and then Jimmy got the sack!

I heard on the grapevine that I was getting the reputation of being a nutcase; I used to get stuck in and get sent off. Anybody who was wanting to have a fight I would stand up and fight with them and I got a reputation. So I really knuckled down. I said, 'There's something for me.' I thought I'd missed the boat, you see, because at 16 if you don't go senior you start wondering. Jim Jefferies came in at Berwick and he brought Billy Brown in and Billy knew me from my Junior days and took a liking to me and that's when I switched on. I really started working hard on my physique and my fitness and I started playing and Jim Jefferies came in one day and said: 'I'm gonna play you at centre-forward.' I says, 'Fine,' and I went up to centre-forward and never looked back. We were the bottom of the League and the team went on a 22-game unbeaten run.

DAVID McGREGOR: One new thing I've had to get used to is dealing with agents and it's part and parcel of football now, even at our level. I think quite a lot of young lads think taking an agent on is a big thing to do but I'm not convinced it does them a lot of good because a lot of agents have never even seen them playing. It's just ridiculous. The SFA chief executive, David Taylor, is a shareholder. His father was a board member and died not long after he got the chief executive's job, but I think still one of his father's proudest moments was about three months after David got the job at the SFA when they both came to a cup tie against Ross County and his father was so proud bringing him into the boardroom, the chief executive of the SFA, the local lad comes home. He often says when he's at our games he has to say to his neighbour: 'You realise I might jump up if Forfar score.'

When we played Rangers in the quarter-final of the Cup at Forfar, someone commented on the fact it was the longest-serving secretary in the Premier League against the longest-serving secretary in the Scottish League: Campbell Ogilvie against myself. I explained what the big difference is: 'Campbell, you've been paid for it for all these years.'

STUART COSGROVE: St Johnstone are one of half a dozen yo-yo clubs, along with Airdrie, Raith Rovers, Falkirk, Morton and St Mirren; their whole history has been moving up and down the divisions in boom-and-bust periods. Saints were close to liquidation once and down to 300 fans. I came home from London and went to a game against Clyde and you were looking at 250 people – dead, dead, dead – and you were wondering what happened to the thousands who used to come and gradually they came back again. I think people support a winning team and when a manager or players manage to capture the imagination of a town.

IAN BLACK: I went to my first Queen of the South game at five years old and my dad took me to home and away games. Since then, and I'm 37 now, I've been to Celtic games and I've been to Rangers games and if Queens haven't been playing I've even been down to Carlisle, but there was never the same feeling going to watch them than going to watch Queens. The 1975–76 season was probably the best season I've ever seen Queens and we actually beat Rangers in the League Cup. They beat us 1–0 at Ibrox and we beat them 2–1 at Palmerston. OK, they scored in extra-time to make it 3–2 on aggregate but it was a moral victory really. The capacity of the ground used to be 20,000 with the biggest crowd maybe 26,000 against Hearts in 1952 in the Scottish Cup. Nowadays the capacity is down to 6,500 and the average gate is about 2,000.

JACK McCONNELL: Because I was on Arran and there were no major football teams around, my uncle, who I used to stay with just outside Wemyss Bay on my summer holidays, took me to Morton on a regular basis and I remember the old Cappielow ground very well. Scandinavian players were just coming into the Scottish leagues and Morton were always in the top five or six in the League, with a very exciting team. So, like everyone else, I caught the bug in the late '60s. We always went to night games, my uncle being a farmer, and the atmosphere at night for a youngster was fantastic. Since then I have always preferred night games to Saturday-afternoon games. I followed Morton for years although it was quite unusual at university when people would ask which football club you supported and I would say 'Morton'. I lived in Stirling for a long, long time and I was very closely involved with the club there, home and away, and those were some of the most enjoyable times I can remember watching football, when they were winning the League and the emotional times when they were moving from their old stadium which had a long history. They built a brand new stadium outside the town and I was on the council at the time and we helped them with that. There was a great community spirit around the club and even the away games with a small number of fans going to Brechin and Arbroath everyone knew each other and it was a great day out. Brechin was always great fun. Stirling Albion fans always treated going to Brechin as a holiday, a beach party, and everyone would dress accordingly. These small clubs are a very important part of our national game but they have suffered over the last 30 years from being too many and what you have are four or five clubs in quite a small geographical area and they can't get the numbers of supporters to make it viable. In the area I lived we had Stirling Albion, Alloa, Falkirk, Stenhousemuir and East Stirling – all in a 15-mile diameter or something like that – and, with the exception of Falkirk, getting small crowds.

JOHN HUGHES: Boys being boys, all the Leith boys said they would come down and watch me at Berwick, so there were about 20 of them came down and the plan was to watch the game and spend the night out at Berwick town centre, get to the disco, and get the bus to come and pick us up later on at night and have a yahoo. But it never went to plan and after one game there was a little bit of a fight broke out and two or three of us got into trouble. Jim Jefferies got to hear about it and on the Monday morning told me he was selling me to Swansea City. It was full-time football, and Beverley and me had not long been married, so I went down to Wales. We settled in Swansea and Beverley came down, then she came back up the road because she couldn't settle. It was easy for me, because I had my football. I was training every day and battering away and it was a great experience. My father would come down, my sister would come down, my brother would come down, all Beverley's family would come down and spend the weekend and things like that. Then Jim Jefferies left Berwick Rangers and went to Falkirk and Terry Yorath called me in at Swansea and says: 'Listen, there's been a bid for you from Falkirk. We've accepted it and we would like you to go and speak to him, go and see what he's got to say and make sure you've got yourself sorted out.'

I just shook his hand and says: 'I'm gone and I'll no' be coming back, my wife's homesick.' So we went up to the flat and we got as much furniture in our wee Suzuki Jeep, seats doon, and took off up the road to Scotland to sign for Falkirk. I had a year's full-time football under me so I was ready for it and I was still a striker. Initially it went terrible for me and there was the boo boys having a go at me and it's a standing joke, now if I'm standing up I say to the Falkirk fans: 'I've got you guys to thank for my football career because if youse didnae boo me as a centre-forward and say "get that big useless bastard back to centre-half" I would never be where I am now!' That's what happened and eventually I've sort of moved to centre-half and I never looked back.

JACK McCONNELL: Stirling Albion had been managed by Alex Smith before he went on to the big time and won his two Scottish Cups with St Mirren and Aberdeen, and then they had John Brogan, who was quite a lively character and a great driving force in the club. Kevin Drinkell was also there, but when they were relegated from the First Division they just couldn't cope financially.

LORD MACFARLANE: That was the period at the end of the war around 1943–4 when there were some great players at Hampden. Unfortunately, when I went into the Army, I had a very bad accident. I had my leg broken and my back broken and so I never really played again. So I'm always able to say that I might have been going to be one of the greats and nobody can argue. When I think of The Strollers forward line that I played in, Walter Waddell played at outside-right, as it was called in these days. He was a good player, he played for Kirkintilloch and then, unfortunately, at Hampden they discovered that he was a reinstated professional and he disappeared. Billy McPhail played in that second team with The Strollers along with a very good player called Jackie Cranston, who went to Airdrie. All super people and all good players and it was a marvellous atmosphere and the lovely thing is, of course, that Queen's Park are still in existence and playing a part in this astonishing game whereas most things of that type have disappeared. Corinthians have all but vanished.

FRANK McAVEETY: I had the misfortune to have two big brothers who were exceptionally good footballers. My oldest brother James was a centre-forward and scored about 70 goals in one season for the school team and he was also a sprinter so I had a lot to follow on from that. My other problem was that my older brother, Philip, was a brilliant football player who ended up signing professional so you were always having to follow in their footsteps and if you did not you were letting the family name down. It was a very competitive environment and I lost two teeth, along with Philip, because of his temper, at a football match. I think that's why he became professional and I didn't. My surname appears in Alex Ferguson's biography. Unfortunately it's my brother, Philip, who was signed by him when Fergie was St Mirren manager. Right all through my adult life people would always say, 'Are you Philip's wee brother?' because football matters in that community and I bet you they're not saying, 'Is that your brother that's the sports minister?'

I was a goalkeeper and all four of us actually played together for the Catholic Boys' Guild, which was quite a good feeling that you actually played in the same team as your three brothers.

Springburn was a fairly mixed community, a combination of both divides in the city, but it didn't matter what background my mates came from, we just played football with them; there was none of this, 'I'll only mix with Celtic supporters'. Historically, everybody in the family has been a Celtic supporter so there's an affection there and certainly when I was growing up Celtic were very successful.

BILL PATERSON: I grew up very close to Parkhead, in Dennistoun. When there was a big game and the wind was in the right direction you could hear the roar from the ground. If you were supporting teams based on your locality I would have been a Celtic supporter, but of course Glasgow didn't allow you to do that. The school I went to governed which team I supported and

Gone but not forgotten: Third Lanark in the early 1960s.
(© *Daily Record*/Mirrorpix)

I went with my dad to Ibrox, across the other side of town. Then we saw a horrible fight once and my dad said 'never again'. It wasn't much of a fight by present-day standards but my dad wasn't interested in that side of football and I reverted to the love of Tilly, my favourite uncle, who was a big Third Lanark supporter and recruited us to their cause. Let's face it, Third Lanark needed all the support they could get. He would take me to Cathkin Park to see what were, I have to admit, some pretty pathetic encounters. But then Third Lanark had a bit of a revival in the early '60s where they had the famous scarlet-and-white line-up in the forwards of Hilley, Harley and Gray, and there were a few brief years when they got within spitting distance of the League and had a couple of good cup runs. Our support for them was beginning to look justified and then, all of a sudden, in the mid-'60s they just vanished. They were relegated at the end of the 1964–65 season and within two years there was a housing estate where Cathkin Park used to be. Even now you can see the remains of the terracing. That was it.

FRANK McAVEETY: I have been reasonably fortunate because I've also been involved in public office so I had a chance when I was Council Leader of Glasgow to meet a lot of people in football and I have also had the good fortune to have played on Firhill, Hampden and Celtic Park in charitable games. What I've never had the chance to do yet, and maybe that's an ambition, is play at Ibrox. Once I played against a team of Church of Scotland ministers and I was playing up the front with Tommy Sheridan and both of us were getting kicked lumps out of. After ten minutes we realised that there's no God's grace with Church of Scotland ministers. They beat us 5–1, the season Celtic won 5–1 against Rangers!

BILL PATERSON: I played football at Whitehill School like every other kid, and for the Boys' Brigade if they were stuck. But I wasn't a great footballer, although I was quite sporty and I still have a book I won in 1957 for being Sportsboy of the Year at school. I ran in the running team and swam in the swimming team. My daughter is different. She is that new breed of young girl who plays football and she turns out for Ham & High Girls in London, so she is the footballer in our family. She certainly didn't get her skills from me. There are an awful lot of people in my profession who are totally hooked on football but I got interested in climbing, a game you couldn't get beaten at. I found the need to escape from Glasgow and with a bus from the city centre you could be in another world in 40 minutes and I couldn't resist that. I think a lot of other young lads found their escape in football and a couple I grew up with, they played at reasonable professional level. One guy, Alex Willoughby, went on to sign for Rangers and was the local superstar, the David Beckham of his time. But then an awful lot of showbusiness people in Scotland reverted to a sort of tattered backing of Partick Thistle, who are the sort of Chelsea of Scotland, with a large celebrity support and they were the team you could support because firstly there was never any sort of fear that they would be exposed at any high level and secondly they took you away from the Old Firm business. The big joke about going to Firhill in those days was that the spectators were introduced to the players rather than the other way round.

CRAIG BROWN: My father was a wing commander in the Royal Air Force. He was a parachute expert and physical training instructor, so my two brothers and I had a stern upbringing. One of the things we were taught was never to show pain. Even if we had broken a leg during a game of football my dad would have preferred it if we had refrained from showing any sign of weakness. My father was a pro player, not at a high level because the war interfered with his career. But he played for Hamilton and Partick Thistle for a spell and King's Park, later to become Stirling Albion. Then he went to RAF Cosford and guested for Wolverhampton. He encouraged all his sons to play golf and football. We stayed in Hamilton, where there was a bit of waste ground by the side of the house, and then played for local school team, St John's Primary, then to secondary school at Hamilton Academy, then the Scottish school team and then Scottish youth team. Dad took me to Hamilton Accies; my uncle took me to Hampden to see Queen's Park.

One of my contemporaries in the school international team was Alex Ferguson, who was a year younger than me. Billy McNeill was in it, too, and he was slighly older. We lost 4–3 to England at Dulwich; the previous year we had beaten them 3–0 at Celtic Park. Alex was a good schoolboy player. I played left-half, Billy was at centre-half and Alex was a striker, and quite an aggressive one, a 'bustling striker' which, of course, is a euphemism for a dirty so-and-so. Alex brought me into the Scotland management set-up and I was a colleague, a friend more than a boss. He was quite laid back and relaxed and had, and has, a great sense of humour. The impression of Alex is as a hard man, but I always say to him: 'You know, Alex, all the men you killed are still alive.' When you have personal friends on the staff – Archie Knox, Walter Smith, Alex and myself – it is a very happy experience. Alex didn't rule with a rod of iron, everything was done as a democracy.

JOHN HUGHES: Some of the things that went on at Falkirk, you couldn't print them. But everything was just fun, fun, fun, right down to the famous one when I ran around the pitch in the nude past Maurice Johnston. Mo was being interviewed when I ran past in the nude, he said, 'Morning', and that was it. Later on I did a Tam Cowan show and I said, 'Right, I'll come on your show as long as you dinnae show that clip because I'm trying to sort of live it down.'

Tam said, 'Fine', but as soon as I went on the show he said: 'I've got a surprise for you,' and there's me running around the pitch.

WILLIE YOUNG: My father was a pretty good player, although never a professional, and he played for Bromley in Kent. He was a civil servant and his work took him there. I had two brothers and we all played. Academically, we were fairly gifted and mother was trying to wean us away from football and in that she succeeded, because we all went to university and football took a back seat. The local club was Girvan Amateurs, one of the oldest senior clubs in the country. An uncle was vice-chairman of Ayr United and that was the nearest team so we went to watch them. As a referee you can't be a fan, but of all the clubs in Scotland they were the only one I can say I have ever supported. That was when Ally McLeod was manager. Ayr were bottom of the old Second Division and Ally kept them in the Premier League for six seasons, maybe more. In the top six of the Premier League, it's almost inconceivable. But he had a very good team with Alex Ingram, Davie Stewart, the goalkeeper, Dick Malone, the full-back who went to Sunderland and won the Cup with them, Spud Murphy, the left-back – a fantastic player and the only reason he never got a Scotland cap was because Danny McGrain was around at the time. Ayr had a half-back line of Sanny McAnespie, who is still in management down in the juniors, Ricky Fleming, a boy they got from Hibs who was a super player and Dougie Mitchell. Up front they had Quinton Young, who went to Rangers and was succeeded by Johnny Doyle, who went to Celtic. It was an exciting wee ground and would be packed for games with the Old Firm, with 20,000-plus supporters.

Dad took me to my first game, a semi-final of the League Cup, in the early '60s and I could barely see over the wall at Hampden because at Hampden they had a sunken enclosure in front of the main stand. That was the first time I had been to Glasgow and it was a big adventure for a small boy.

CRAIG BROWN: I was doing OK but had five operations and the left knee got knackered. I am not saying I would have been a superstar, but I believe I would have done a whole lot better. My only regret is I had to more or less give up playing golf because of the arthritis and I had a handicap of four.

JOHN HUGHES: When Jim Jefferies left Falkirk to go to Hearts he phoned me up and asked me if I wanted to go to Tynecastle and I told him I was going to Celtic. He says: 'I'll match anything, I want to bring you to Hearts,' and I says, 'No, I cannae.' He understood that Celtic was too much. Bill McMurdo was my agent, Agent Orange as they call him, and I was sat with him when the phone rang. Bill McMurdo told me it was Tommy Burns for me. I thought it was a wind-up, but this guy says: 'I'm looking to bring you to Parkhead, to Celtic, what do you think about it?'

'Aye, aye, great,' I said, still thinking it was a wind-up, but eventually I twigged.

Tommy says: 'Are you keen to come?'

I went: 'Who wouldnae be?'

Bill organises to meet him that night, him and Billy Stark and we done the deal and I went into Celtic on the Saturday when they were playing Newcastle in a friendly and Rod Stewart was opening the new stand. So I says, 'How are you doing?' to Rod Stewart, watched the Newcastle game, came in on the Monday, signed my forms, done all my press and I made my debut against Liverpool against Robbie Fowler and Ian Rush.

My father hadn't seen me playing for a while and he came to my debut and I ran out in front of about 40,000 with the biggest smile on, as if to say, 'This is what I've worked so hard for, this is for me.' There were nae nerves. 'This is for me. This is where I want to be.' We drew 0–0.

WILLIE YOUNG: I played morning, noon and night with my two brothers and then I captained the school's team and Ayrshire schools team and we went down to Manchester to play Manchester Schools and to Cumbria. At 15 or 16 some teams were watching me, but I would have never had the pace to last at senior level, that's a family failing. Greg, my younger brother, played as a professional. He was a goalkeeper for Clyde and he was very good, but me and my other brother John can claim some credit for that, because when we were kids Greg, as the youngest, was put in goals; we wouldn't let him play out. Craig Brown signed him for Clyde and Alex Ferguson had him on trial at St Mirren when he was there. Craig rated him very highly but Greg wouldn't take it seriously – he's a laugh-a-minute guy and doesn't take anything seriously. So Craig didn't think he was applying himself, but he played the entire season they won the Second Division Championship. Jock Stein, the Scotland manager at the time, wanted to cap him at Under-21 level but Brown said: 'No, I'll tell him you were going to cap him but unless he gets his attitude right . . .' They tried to use it as a spur, but it didn't bother Greg, he just carried on as normal.

Work took him down to Newcastle and he started playing at amateur level for Whitley Bay and Tow Law Town and he was involved in an hilarious penalty incident in the FA Cup with Whitley Bay which was televised. The two teams had played 120

minutes in horrendous conditions over two games and it came
down to penalty kicks to decide who would go into the next
round of the FA Cup. The guy who was taking the kick against
Greg ran up and just as he got to the ball took cramp, fell forward
and headed the ball off the spot. It went about two yards, Greg
jumped out of goals and picked up the ball and told the referee:
'I'm a qualified referee. That's the kick taken and we're through.'
The ref was a bit flustered by this and said: 'Quite right.'

In fact, you can't take a penalty kick with your head – the ball
has to be kicked. But it's a bit late now!

LAURA HIRD: My dad Ronnie used to go to Tynecastle on his
own and leave me, my mum and my granny talking over a bacon
roll or to go shopping on a Saturday. My mum said I wasn't allowed
to go because men peeed into beer bottles and all that sort of thing.
I remember rainy, winter nights with people in the streets heading
for the ground. Dad was a passionate Hearts fan when he could still
afford to go, but a few years ago he was made redundant from his
job with Allied Breweries at Sighthill and had to content himself
with listening to matches on the radio. He found it difficult after
that because he never had a season ticket. When I got a job I would
buy him tickets to go and by then it had probably been 29 years
since he had been to see Hearts. Now there was a completely new
team and they were playing in Europe and things like that. My
mum just tolerated it. She thought it was indulgence but it was my
dad's only real passion, that and an occasional flutter on the horses.
I went to Tynecastle School, and I was at school with John
Robertson's ex-wife, but it's sinful to say I have never been to
Tynecastle. I took a liking to Raith Rovers when I was seeing a man
from Kirkcaldy who was a Raith Rovers fan and went to Stark's
Park where I would occasionally see Hearts play Raith Rovers!
Rovers were in their big year with Jimmy Nicholl as manager and
they won the Coca-Cola Cup, beating Celtic in the final, so it was
quite exciting following them. I even got to go to the civic

reception in Kirkcaldy. I remember one paper saying, 'They'll be dancing in the streets of Raith tonight!' We went to a karaoke and Jimmy Nicholl and some of the players were there singing and I went up and congratulated him. Gordon Dalziel was there, too. I saw Rangers at Stark's Park, and Celtic, and I was quite starstruck because there you are watching Gascoigne, Laudrup and McCoist and people like that.

Rovers are not doing so well now but a few of that team moved on to Rangers or Celtic and got in the Scotland team. I still have a soft spot for them. I went to see them playing Bayern Munich and stood with the Bayern fans, which was great.

WILLIE YOUNG: I got injured, a terrible injury when the kneecap went round the side of my leg and caused all sorts of damage, and I realised I wouldn't be able to play again. Saturdays without football? Too awful to contemplate, so Louis Thau Jnr said: 'Why don't you try refereeing?'

I said he had to be kidding, because I was the world's worst with referees when I played. I couldn't do that, I couldn't take all that abuse.

But I tried it and I progressed and although it was only a hobby and a way of occupying myself on a Saturday I got on the line. The SFA sent me to a UEFA Cup match, Nantes v. Torino, when the referee was David Syme. The boy who came to Hearts, Pasquale Bruno, was playing for Torino and I think David put off a couple of players. But the experience of my first-ever trip to Europe was what changed my views. You were looked after brilliantly: club-class travel, five-star hotels, and it was fantastic to be involved at that level. I came back from that trip and lost over a stone through increased training and changing my eating habits.

JOHN HUGHES: When I first went to Hibs, Jocky Scott signed me from Celtic. I didn't want to leave Celtic, but they had just signed Alan Stubbs so the writing was on the wall and I always wanted to play for Hibs. Even in my Falkirk days every summer I was with the Hibs in the close season.

I used to travel with Gordon Marshall back to Edinburgh and what a laugh we used to have, what a laugh. I got a car from a mate of mine who had a garage, it was a big Ford Sierra Ghia and me and Marsh used to call it the Bobsleigh; this thing was computerised. We could skate around corners, this thing would go anywhere and you could do handbrake turns and oh, the laughs we used to get in it. It never let us down, hammering it up and down the motorway all the time.

CRAIG BROWN: My Rangers career was very unillustrious, that's the best way to describe it. I was 17 when I signed for them and they farmed me out for a year to Coltness Juniors, near Wishaw. Now junior football was for the old hard men but I was a young hard man and I could compete with them. I played in Rangers reserves with some famous players like Johnny Hubbard, Ian McCall, Davie Provan, Ronnie McKinnon, Willie Henderson. The following year I was still in the reserves, and Bob Shankly took me on loan to Dundee for six months and at the end of the loan period Bob signed me for an undisclosed fee reputed to be £8,000. I never played in the Rangers first team.

Craig Brown in Dundee colours, 1962.
(© *Sunday Mail*)

WILLIE YOUNG: I reffed the Junior Cup final in 1990 and was then promoted to Class One. The higher you go in football the easier it gets. The only downside is the media. My wife basically cancelled the newspapers; she gets the *Sunday Post*, the only paper that never criticises referees. I am thick-skinned, although I have been known to ring up writers and tell them they have got it wrong. Not that an apology was ever going to appear in print the next day. I do remember getting a game on the line at Wembley when England played Brazil and the ref was Jim McCluskey. We flew down, were in Whites Hotel on Bayswater Road. A car came for us, a limo, and I don't mean one of those vulgar American things, I mean a thing like a hearse with a three-inch deep carpet. We were shown into this limo by the Whites doorman, who was all suited up, and then we were driving up Wembley with 80,000 people on the way to the ground, plus more media than I've ever seen. People were peering in through the window and I was getting really nervous, and I said to Jim: 'This is incredible.' I remembered then my early days refereeing the College League on Glasgow Green, where they had 20 or 30 pitches on a Saturday morning. The kick-off was about 10 a.m. and the players were always late because they had been out the night before. There were 15 referees in this communal changing-room and I recall this wee Glasgow Corporation guy coming on and putting his hat on to tell us: 'If you're no' oot they pitches by 12, I'm throwing your claes oot.' I related that story on the way up Wembley Way. What a contrast!

There were a few Scottish-based players in the England team – Terry Butcher, Trevor Steven and Gary Stevens – and they invited us into the England dressing-room and we got some autographs, which you shouldn't really do, but there you go. It was great, apart of course from chalking off the winning Brazil goal. It was 1–1 and Brazil did a one–two and it looked clearly offside so I flagged and nobody batted an eyelid at the time. But then at night Jimmy Hill got his sliderule out to prove the player was a yard onside so it was a bad decision – and because it was England it was one I took an awful lot of ribbing for.

SAMMY THE TAMMY: I am eight years old and was born when the club decided they were going to have a mascot. They decided they would have a competition and asked the young supporters' club to design an outfit. Then this company down south, Rainbow Productions, made this vision come to life as a proper mascot. It was actually a young girl who won the competition and the thing she drew looked a little like a bear and it was called Sammy the Tammy. The key thing is to give it a personality, otherwise it's just a suit. From the very first day we have kept it a closely guarded secret who is inside, mainly because of the Santa Claus effect for kids. We want the kids to believe it is a real animal and it lives. I know that sounds bizarre but for kids it's real. The other aspect is we watched with pure disbelief when Hearts allowed Ally McCoist to wear their suit and then take the head off. Then for about three or four seasons after, folk on the Heart of Midlothian terraces would say: 'I wonder who's in the suit today. Is it Ally McCoist again?'

The person inside became more an issue than the mascot itself. What we wanted was for the mascot to take the lead and if we ever had to change the person inside then no one would know any differently.

Bear necessities: Sammy the Tammy entertains the crowd. (Photo courtesy of Dunfermline FC)

I do have an understudy, and it's very important because there are holidays and things like that. I haven't missed many matches in eight years and my understudy studies me very closely and tries to copy everything I do. It's not so bad at a home game because there is a sort of set routine that we do, but it's more difficult when you are out and about at galas and things like that.

WILLIE YOUNG: I actually thought that running the line was more difficult than being a referee, because you have a restricted view and the speed of the players at that level is phenomenal. You are also a lot closer to the crowd, of course, so I have had gob-stoppers and pies thrown at me, and on one occasion, at Easter Road, a railway sleeper bolt. One time at the old Airdrie ground where there was a raised wooden stand so the crowd were about 15 feet above the ground someone threw a battery at my linesman. This guy had been listening to the radio and had become so infuriated he had taken them out and flung them at the linesman. He wanted me to report it to the police, which I did, and the senior police officer said: 'Oh, that'll be assault and battery then?'

SAMMY THE TAMMY: It's hot inside that outfit, and the worst scenario is a hot sunny day for something like the civic parade because you're inside then for two or three hours and the health and safety regulations stipulate 45 minutes. I get totally dehydrated and there is no air and many a time a young kid's come up to me and said: 'You are smelly.' There is a rivalry with other mascots but to be honest there is such a turnover of mascots it's hard to keep up with them. We used to be friends with Hearty Harry at Tynecastle but of course he has been withdrawn; he doesn't do it any more. There was a lot of rivalry with the guy who did Paisley Panda when Pars and St Mirren were both vying for the same promotion spot. Bruce, up at Aberdeen, who does Angus the Bull is a good guy. I do get stick from opposing fans, some players too. Paul Gascoigne always used to give us a kick on the way past, just for fun.

Sammy is getting a bit tatty. He's eight years old and we have been on at the club to get a new suit. The new one is on order and it should look identical, but those who have studied Sammy over the years may notice a few differences.

JOHN HUGHES: The three-year contract at Hibs gave me the security. I always stayed in Leith and it was only two minutes up the road from me, so I dived at it; it was a good deal and I grabbed it. It was always an ambition of mine to play for my club and it was a greater honour for me when I got to be the captain and great disappointment when they got relegated. That's the worst I've ever been when I got relegated for Hibs, because as I say I'm out and about in Leith and it's all Hibs supporters that are there and I sort of hid in the house for a couple of weeks. I really took it hard, but you have to get yourself back up and Alex McLeish came in and we bounced right back up.

It was a great year winning the First Division then we got guys like Franck Sauzee, big Mixu Paatelainen and Grant Brebner.

John Hughes celebrates Hibs' Skol Cup win in 1992.
(© *Daily Record*/Mirrorpix)

SAMMY THE TAMMY: I am from Alloa originally and my father took me to a Scottish Cup match against Aberdeen, who had guys like Drew Jarvie at the time. I was nine or ten and I can remember the day very clearly because there was a riot at half-time and Ally

McLeod, who was manager, came out with a loudhailer and pleaded with everyone to get off the park and let us finish the game.

Half of the problem was the riot and the other half the fog that was coming in and obscuring the pitch. My father said, 'Right, I'm not taking you to another game again.' My great-great-grandfather was actually the coach at one time. My dad, not being a football man, thought he had to get everything sorted so he had a flask and sandwiches and all that sort of stuff. He wasn't really a football man.

I have always believed in supporting your local team and when I got a job in Dunfermline, around 1988, it was permissible to be half Alloa and half Dunfermline but of course after a few games of going to see the Pars the Alloa thing got dropped.

LAURA HIRD: It's funny, but I have never been able to get away from football. I was brought up near Tynecastle and when I was in London I lived near White Hart Lane and then moved to a place near Highbury. When I moved back to Edinburgh I got a place in McLeod Street! I must like it!

JOHN LAMBIE: I played in the school team at Whitburn and was playing under-15 football at 12 years old. I was a centre-forward and moved to Edinburgh Athletic and that was a time when there were some smashing players around – Willie Henderson, Alan Gordon, Tommy Murray, I could go on and on. Willie played for Edinburgh and was some player at 16; he walked into the Rangers side at 16. I'm friendly with Willie yet. He's got a pub in Uphall.

I got a chance to go down to England, but I was a home bird. My mum and dad had a shop in Glasgow just off of Dobbies Loan in Maitland Street and I got a trial here for Partick. I went to Parkhead and spoke to Jimmy McGrory, but I wouldn't sign for them. I just felt if I was going to make the grade I would start in a lower league. I made up my own mind; a lot of them go with their dad but I made up my own mind. My father wouldn't talk to me for two weeks because of that.

JOHN HUGHES: When I left Hibs I was contemplating retiring but I still felt fit as a fiddle. Ayr United came in and they were showing a lot of ambition. They signed Paul Lovering and Michael Renwick, both of whom had been released from Hibs, and James Grady and Eddie Annan, and we felt we had a chance of winning the First Division. But it was really some trek and I tried everything. I tried going down at six o'clock in the morning, I tried going down there at ten o'clock at night and staying over, staying in an hotel, staying over a couple of nights. Ayr United took care of everything like that, but I found it really hard the first year, so much so that I felt maybe the next year I would be better just walking away from it. I was really close to calling it a day and I phoned up Gordon Dalziel and we agreed to give it another year. I worked hard in the pre-season and we had a great year: we got in the semi-final of the Scottish Cup, the final of the CIS Cup. I don't think Ayr United, and no disrespect, I don't think they'll ever do that again, we'll go down in the history books as doing that. I was captain and it was a great year, playing the Old Firm back-to-back and beating my old team Hibs 1–0 in the semi-final of the CIS Cup. But that's football. Football flings up things like that.

JOHN LAMBIE: I know I was harum-scarum and fell out with managers, but I was a good pro. I can mind we were playing Stenhousemuir in a reserve game midweek and a boy called Harry Glasgow took a bad knock and was carried off and they gave me a shout to go to right-back and that was it. I stayed there. It is a lot easier playing there as the game's in front of you.

My biggest disappointment was when I went to St Johnstone and became the first tribunal case in Scotland. Geordie Miller was my best mate and he was at Falkirk at the time. We were hanging around waiting to be shouted in to see Willie Cunningham for signing-on talks and they called Geordie in. He came back out and said: 'That's me signed on for another year.' I went up and the manager said: 'I can't keep two headbangers, one of youse will have to go.' So I said I'd just seen Geordie so it was obvious it was me. I thought I was a free but he said no, we're wanting a fee for you, I think it was about £10,000. Eleven years service for that! I fought my case and won it at Park Gardens. I hadn't played for three weeks but I had kept fit because I had greyhounds and I walked them. I came back from the tribunals went in the house, put the clogs on and took the dogs out. When I came back Willie Ormond was sitting in the house. He wanted to sign me for St Johnstone. I couldn't come to an agreement over terms but eventually I got what I wanted. Then Cunningham told me Rangers had been interested in me!

But I had a great time at St Johnstone, seven great years there. We played against Real Madrid, beat SV Hamburg 3–0 in Europe, went to Budapest and they played me as sweeper. We went there with a 1–0 lead and there was no scoring. Next game was Sarajevo and I got injured in training and they gave us a turning over.

St Johnstone's old ground was one of the best grounds in Scotland and Willie Ormond, with his buck teeth, was a different kind of manager, one of these who liked you to roll up your sleeves and get stuck in. Skill will take care of itself, he said. I've used that myself.

I've only ever read one book apart from football books and pigeon books and that was when I was in getting an operation on my knee and that was *Peyton Place*. I only read it because it was there. I've read every football book going.

I was very fortunate, and only had two injuries. One of them I wasn't even playing. You had to get a job preseason in those days because your wages were down by half when you weren't playing, and I got a job with the Co-operative driving and debt-collecting. I stepped off a lorry into a hole and did all the ankle ligaments, shattered them. That was the worst, although the arthritis is into the knee now. See the bad weather? It's terrible. Honey and cider vinegar is one of cheapest remedies and the best and I've put one or two of the players on it. A herbalist I was seeing for my pigeons put me on it. Cider vinegar, honey and garlic kills off viruses, keeps everything away. The acid in it cleanses your bowels, too. Wee Danny Lennon, I told him about it, and he swears by it. He's been on it ever since.

IAIN PAXTON: I was actually born in Dunfermline, but I have absolutely no allegiance to the Pars. In my formative years they were quite high up and doing well in Europe, but nothing clicked for me. In 1963, when I moved to Burntisland, someone I knew through the church got me thinking about Raith Rovers and when we moved to Ramsay Road, just round the corner from the ground, we were virtually in the shadow of Stark's Park, a couple of hundred yards away. You would wander round the corner and see this football stadium, it could have been the biggest stadium in the world for all I knew. Evening games were even more mystical when you would see the lights above the streets.

I remember match days vividly, although I was too young, at five or six, to be going to matches as far as my folks were concerned. We used to go round the streets on match days counting all the cars because in those days there were not many cars around and on football days it was amazing how many suddenly appeared, fancy cars belonging to the city slickers. My dad was duty sergeant and then chief inspector and he would always go to the football. He was in control of the policing, but I never ever got in the back door. By the time I was nine or ten I got a season ticket for the next three years until I started playing sport on a Saturday afternoon. In the late '60s Rovers got back into the old First Division and they had a cracking season when Gordon Wallace was playing for them and he got the Player of the Year award, which was unheard of for a player from a provincial team. He moved on to Dundee after that one fantastic season and he was my hero, but then again it's anyone who scores goals who you admire, not the guy who saves them.

Gordon was about six foot tall and quite skilful and he had that innate ability to be in the right place at the right time.

In Kirkcaldy, like every other central belt provincial town, there was always a line of buses leaving the esplanade on a Saturday morning and heading for Glasgow. Kirkcaldy and some of that East Fife area was a bit of a Glasgow overspill and they had never lost support for the Old Firm. Rovers had to rely on a hardcore of locals, maybe a solid 2,000–3,000 would always turn up, even in the hard times.

PATRICK BARCLAY: I was born in London but brought to Dundee as a toddler and the first game I saw was 1957 or '58 and it was a 1–0 win against Hibs. The Hibs goalkeeper was Tommy Younger, who I think went on to become president of the SFA, as well as playing for Liverpool and I remember him being in goal.

My grandfather took me there and basically just left me at Dens Park, which you could do in those days. He had been a fan but lost interest although he used to tell me stories about players like Herbert Dainty, who had played in the Cup-winning team of 1910. I was smitten and I just fell in love with Dundee football club and the dark blue shirts. I was living in Blackness Road near the playing fields of the Harris Academy, so walking to the ground was not an option and it was always a bus. The good times arrived straight away so I was lucky. I had only been supporting the team three, three and a half years when they won the Championship. At first they always seemed to be fourth but there was never an option of supporting the other lot because their ground, Tannadice, was little better than a Dundee junior ground. We used to laugh at the place with the little stand and all that.

FORDYCE MAXWELL: The '50s was the great era of Newcastle which was effectively my local team, apart from Berwick. They won the FA Cup three times in five years but the first player who made an impression on me was Bert Trautman, the Manchester City goalkeeper in the 1956 final when he played the last 20 minutes with a broken neck. That was the first game I listened to on the radio back home on the farm. It seems to be at around ten or eleven when most kids become fans. Another great hero when I was eleven or twelve was Duncan Edwards, the Manchester United player who died at Munich; if I could have been any footballer it would have been Duncan Edwards. After that I became almost obsessive about football and there was a period after that where I became the sort of Leslie Welch of our area. In 1957 my uncle Dave took me down to St James' Park for the first time, to see Newcastle against West Brom, and every Christmas or New Year we would go down to see either Newcastle or Sunderland and I remember seeing Sunderland the day Brian Clough broke his leg.

HUGH WALLACE: I lived from the age of five in Queens Drive, so visits to Cathkin Park and Hampden to support the Glasgow teams were commonplace. I recall at the age of eight climbing the wall at Cathkin with another six boys to get in free and being escorted away by the policemen on duty. I was at a Queen's Park v. Celtic match at Hampden in the Scottish Cup, around 1966. Celtic won 1–0, with a goal in the 66th minute. We found ourselves at the Celtic end, so when the goal came our lack of enthusiasm was spotted by a friendly Celtic supporter; he wisely advised us to jump up and down with the rest of the support if we wished to get out alive. It was one of the times when I felt that principles might be prudently foregone in favour of survival. The first time I went to Ibrox, I remember asking my dad if there might be any other people who supported Rangers there. Such is the wonderful naivety and innocence of youth. A number of my own church members are season ticket holders, so attending the matches keeps me in touch with them, as well as the faithful hordes who turn up rain, hail or shine, win, lose or draw at home and away games. I baptised the two children of new president

David Gordon here; the previous president, Kenny Harvey, I married his son just a few weeks ago, so there have been those sort of associations and link-ups.

FORDYCE MAXWELL: The ground has changed a bit. There was a time when there was no roof on the stand for several seasons and like a lot of lower-division clubs they tend to stagger from one crisis to the next. The Rangers game is the one everyone remembers, but actually the best spell for Berwick was in the late '70s and early '80s under Dave Smith, when he actually took them into the First Division. In their promotion season they were pulling in average crowds of 1,200 but, of course, they didn't have the players or resources to maintain it.

HUGH WALLACE: Mount Florida is a community in itself, a village and at one time was the edge of Glasgow. There's a picture of the old changing room at Lesser Hampden, the church and a farm haystack, from 1910, so that was less than 100 years ago.

BOB CRAMPSEY: In 1937 there were crowds of 149,000 and six-figure crowds were normal. I was allowed to go on my own to the replay of the 1938 Scottish Cup final. There were 88,000 there and they passed the kids down to the front in those days and they looked after me very well, sitting me on a crash barrier and giving me an American cream soda; I thought East Fife were a great side! They beat Kilmarnock after extra-time and are still the only Second Division side to win the Cup. Kilmarnock had just been under the management of Jimmy McGrory and they were doing very well until full-time and then Jimmy came out with his hat on to do his team talk and they lost 4–2 so I have always distrusted team talks since.

At that time the city of Glasgow had the best public transport in the world and all round the Queen's Park recreation there would be 150 to 200 trams. You could go as far as Bearsden one way and

Hibs v. Clyde Scottish Cup final at a packed Hampden in 1958. Captains
Eddie Turnbull (Hibs) and Harry Haddock shake hands before kick-off.
Clyde won the match 1–0. (© The Scotsman Publications Limited)

Coatbridge the other; the longest was Airdrie to Renfrew which
was something like 26 miles.

I can give you any First Division side from the '30s but I
couldn't give you the Kilmarnock side from last Saturday's
Scottish Cup final if my life depended on it. Players move more
so they don't form the bond with supporters they once did.

I have a strong connection with Queen's Park and Frank, my
brother, was goalkeeper there for a couple of years. The great
error Queen's made was that they wouldn't join the league in
1890 and there is a wonderful letter from the president saying
'Our biggest objection to the league is that it exists'. As a result
Queen's drifted around for ten years, having to play pick-up
matches and friendlies. They never really recovered from that.

It was a very common and healthy south side thing; you were
a Queen's Park supporter but went to Third Lanark on alternate
Saturdays or vice versa. It was a very sane and sensible way of

watching football. You could have a situation as late as the 1960s when you could wander into Shawfield to watch a game and there would be four Scottish internationals in the Clyde side. If you went to Cathkin a few years earlier you could see Jimmy Mason and Bobby Mitchell. There is no chance of that now.

GORDON SHERRY: I bought my boy Thomas a season ticket to make sure he is a Killie supporter. My brother Ian and my dad were big Killie fans, but originally I used to go with my papa because Dad was in the police and wasn't able to go. We stood at the back of the terracing and what struck me was the Johnnie Walker stand and the big steps up into Rugby Park on to the terracing. The games I really remember were the 1987 Scottish Cup replays with Hearts. In those days there was no extra-time and penalties. Hearts beat us in the third game. It had been 0–0 at Tynecastle, 1–1 at Rugby Park and then it was 3–1 at Rugby Park, and I was at that game with a broken leg after an accident skiing on a golf course.

BOB CRAMPSEY: It's a great loss that footballers these days live in well-off enclaves, a bit reminiscent of Johannesburg. They used to live in the same street as the fans.

When I first went to Hampden we were the football capital of the world and could make that claim right up to the 1950s, with four grounds capable of taking 40,000 or more.

You judged boys you hadn't met by their footballing skills. If they could play football that was good enough. This new chap in the gang could have been St Francis of Assisi, but if he didn't play football nobody wanted to know.

GORDON SHERRY: I wanted to play. I wanted to be a goalkeeper but a broken leg ended it. My hero was my uncle Bill, who played in goal for St Johnstone, Stirling, Partick Thistle and Luton. Bill Taylor is a bit of a legend at Saints. It was quite funny because when I was at university in Stirling I was friends with a guy called Arthur Cameron, who was a big Saints fan, and one day we were talking football and I said my uncle used to play in goal for St Johnstone and he said: 'Not Billy Taylor? Oh, my God, the best goalkeeper who ever played for St Johnstone.'

Bill also gave me lots of tips about golf.

JIM LEISHMAN: Lochgelly, where I was born, is famous for the Lochgelly strap that teachers used. It was a mining town and my father was a miner. He was a Fifer. My mother was from the Borders and she supported Hibs, as did my grandfather and all my uncles. Dad, however, was a Rangers man and he was down the pits when there was a cave-in and he was involved and lost his thumb and broke his leg. When he woke up the first thing he asked the nurses was the Rangers score. Rangers were playing Real Madrid and they got beat 6–1 so that was a bad day for Dad. He wasn't a true-blue Rangers fan, that was just his team until I started getting involved with Dunfermline. They used to go on the Dunfermline supporters bus and if I had any spare tickets I would give them to my father and he would give them to the supporters on the bus so they wouldn't charge him for going on the bus. That was his business venture.

IAN WILSON: I was born in Northfield in Aberdeen, a council scheme. My mother has not long left there, after 50 years and me and my two brothers were all brought up there. I was Aberdeen through and through. I was there as a kid, an apprentice, and I signed at 14. I went full-time at 16 and was there two years, but was released because of my height and lack of strength. That can be a problem; Aberdeen had the opportunity to take Shaun Maloney, but he was too small, apparently. For me, it was an opportunity to prove people wrong. Jimmy Boswell signed me for Aberdeen and Ally McLeod freed me. Physically I wasn't ready for it, Ally told me, and he said a few people had made enquiries about me and blah blah blah but the upshot was I had to go and fend for myself. But you learn quickly and it shows strength and determination and I was pleased I was able to pick myself up because it could have gone the other way.

In the short time I was in the Highland League people started looking at me and in 1979–80 I got the chance to go to Leicester, who were Division Two at the time and had only just managed to avoid relegation. They got a result at Preston to stay up. Jock Wallace was the manager and he came up to see me, and watched me in a couple

Fox on the run: Ian Wilson made his name with Leicester City. (Photo courtesy of Peterhead FC)

of games. They took me down to Leicester just after my 21st birthday, kept me out of sight and wouldn't let anyone else get near me. They paid Elgin £30,000 which is still one of the biggest transfer fees in the Highland League. I went to Everton for £300,000 in 1987 after Leicester got relegated. I had got myself into the Scotland team while I was at Leicester and I wanted to see if I could maintain that and turned down a move, or it fell through, to Luton Town. Then I got a call to go and see the Leicester manager, Brian Hamilton, after a game in which we beat Plymouth 4–1 and I'd played really well. Brian said: 'Howard Kendall and Colin Harvey will be ringing this office any minute from Everton,' and sure enough they did.

JIM LEISHMAN: In 1968, George Farm signed me for Dunfermline and they had just won the Cup. They beat Celtic in the first round and Hearts in the final. They were very successful in Europe, and reached the semi-final of the Cup-Winners' Cup in 1969. The halcyon days, as they call it.

Then they had a very poor decade when the Premier League reconstruction was going on and the Pars lost a generation of supporters at that time because of the poor results.

I was a trialist at 15 but you got shoved into the under-18 age groups, you never played people your own age. They made you play older ones to see how you would handle it. Because I got in the first team quickly, at 17, I was working hand-in-hand with senior players and got a lot of help and encouragement and advice but you also got told off when you had to be told off. You got a slap on the head when you stepped out of line.

ERIC MILLIGAN: I was brought up in the Hearts faith. I am 53 and many things have changed in my life, but the one constant has been my devotion to Hearts. If you meet anyone with a greater fervour you'll have done well. I was born in 1951 in Robertson Avenue. My grandmother, my father's mother, lived at 172 Gorgie Road, which is above the savings bank and her windows looked into Tynecastle Lane. My father was a devoted Hearts fan and so were my uncles.

The post-war years were the high watermark for British football. With the introduction of football on a Saturday afternoon, working men were looking for something to do; they had money in their pockets and the numbers that were going to matches in the post-war years were greater than before or since. That was the Britain, the Edinburgh I grew up in. It was also a time when the two Edinburgh clubs were genuinely competing against Rangers and Celtic. During the 1950s Hibs were Scottish League champions three times and Hearts won it twice and they won a number of League Cups, too. That has never happened before or since.

ALEX TOTTEN: Since I have been able to walk I have played football because that was the done thing then. Every Christmas I got a ball, a pair of boots and a tin of dubbin. Everyone played, morning, noon and night, with the jackets down and 16 or 20 a side. My mother went to the headmaster at primary school and he asked her what I wanted to do when I left school and she said that I wanted to be a professional footballer. He said: 'Aye, they all want to be that.'

But I achieved my ambition. Denny High School picked me for Scottish Schools, and it was a record for Stirlingshire because there were four lads picked: Davie Catanach, Willie Smith, Ian Mitchell and myself. We played England, Ireland and Wales, and beat all three to win the Victory Shield.

There were lots of scouts at games like that and I went to Manchester United with my parents because they wanted to sign me. I was 15 and it was the first time I had been in an aeroplane. I met Bobby Charlton, who was my hero. I also went to Middlesbrough and Birmingham but eventually signed for Liverpool because of one man, Bill Shankly. Ian St John signed in the June, I signed in July and big Ron Yeats signed in August; it was that era.

I was an apprentice professional and was paid £13 a week and the digs money had to come out of that. I thought it was great; all the money went into Barclays Bank in Liverpool and after about three months the bank manager called me in and said: 'You owe us.'

I was quite fortunate because there were four Scottish lads in the same digs and they showed me the ropes. It was a tremendous education and not just in the football sense because we used to go to The Cavern and see The Beatles and The Swinging Blue Jeans, groups like that, and Cilla White as she was then. One night we came home to the digs and we were listening to Radio Luxembourg and one of the guys said: 'That's that group, what are they called? The Beatles?' It was a great time in Liverpool in the '60s.

I never made the first team but I had a great four years there. Tommy Smith and I were on the groundstaff together and even at 16 he was a wonderful player. He was always knocking on Shanks's door: 'I want the first team,' and Shanks would tell him to bide his time. Then one day in five-a-side he crocked Chris Lawler and he was off to Shanks's house: 'Will I be in the team on Saturday?' I speak at dinners and tell a lot of Shankly stories.

He was a great man and very, very witty. It was a great place for football education, cleaning The Kop, the baths and the boots. When I became a manager I used to tell Skillseekers: 'I'm never going to ask you to do anything I haven't done myself,' and of course it's true.

ARTHUR MONTFORD: The sports jacket was, quite honestly, largely a myth. I did have one or two light, cheery jackets but I felt it was part of the persona of *Scotsport*, bright, cheerful and just ordinary guys were doing this programme. We had fun. The most outrageous of the jackets was sold at a Help The Aged auction in Dundee many years after I stopped wearing it and they got some very, very high figure for it – over £100. Some football nutter wanted to be wearing that but it went to a good cause eventually. So the jacket that cost a tenner actually made a huge profit.

ALEX TOTTEN: My father liked football and he would come down on the bus to see me at Liverpool. Grandfather was a great Falkirk man and that's where the Falkirk thing came in. When they won the Scottish Cup in 1957, I went to every game although I was only 11. Alex Parker was my idol. He went to Everton and when I went to Liverpool I couldn't wait to play against him and tell him: 'You were my hero.' Eventually Shanks took me in and told me it hadn't worked out and 'because I let you go doesn't mean you won't make it elsewhere'. It was hard to take because the usual route was Liverpool first team, Scotland B, then maybe a Scotland cap. My mother met me at Glasgow Central and I felt like a failure but it has happened to thousands of lads and will happen to thousands more. I went to Dundee and so played under both Shanklys. I made my debut with Jocky Scott who had come up from Chelsea and we beat Motherwell 6–0. On Saturday we played Rangers and I was up against Willie Henderson; Alan Cousin was against Bobby Shearer – it was like the old against the young. I remember Jim Baxter came in the dressing-room beforehand – he knew Hammy and Alan Gilzean from playing for Scotland and said: 'Bet you 50 quid we beat you.' We beat them 4–1 and next Saturday we went to Dundee United and beat them 4–1. I always remember the newspaper saying: 'And Dundee's merited win can be traced to that great defensive trio of Hamilton, Wright and Totten'! There were a lot of smashing players there.

I remember Gilzean said one Friday at lunch: 'That's it, lads, I don't care if I break my leg tomorrow because I'm off to Tottenham.' And he was; £72,500, that's what he went for.

ARTHUR MONTFORD: One of the great things about joining STV was the way television developed, and how we developed. Film gave way to video tape, video tape became more sophisticated and nowadays the commentators have slow-motion replays, different angles, you see the ball in flight and you can almost see the name on it as it hits the post; it's unbelievable. The technical advancement in sports coverage has been phenomenal and it must be an absolute joy to be a commentator now with all that expertise and facilties. We had to hold a microphone, shuffle our notes, and the snow and the rain were coming in through the roof. The change has been dramatic.

ALEX TOTTEN: I had five years at Dunfermline under Willie Cunningham. Jock Stein had just left to go to Hibs. We were always in Europe and they were a great bunch of lads with no cliques. We won the Cup in 1968, George Farmer took over as manager, and after that went over to America with Manchester City to try and promote the game there. Five weeks we were away – Los Angeles, New York, Vancouver and Toronto – and it was great for a young boy of 22 or 23. Joe Mercer was City manager, Malcolm Allison his assistant and they had players like Franny Lee, Mike Summerbee and Tony Book. Fergie played for us then, of course. We were down at Kilmarnock and I was up against Tommy McLean and we drew 2–2 and it was a great game. The replay was at East End Park and Fergie, who was noted for only scoring inside the 18-yard box, scored a 25-yarder, beating Bobby Ferguson (who went to West Ham) and we won 1–0.

When we beat Aberdeen George Farm told me I had to look after Jinky Smith and next day the headlines said: 'Totten Subdues Smith'!

ARTHUR MONTFORD: I was very lucky that I made friends with players, managers and supporters of all clubs. I was welcome at every ground in Scotland, which I always regarded as a great tribute to the professional work that I did. People could see that I loved the game. It was obvious that I was a Morton supporter and that I had no great affiliations elsewhere. I reported objectively on every game and if it was a poor match I said so; if I thought it was a bad game I said so and I gave praise when it was due and I was welcomed by fans, officials, players and managers at every ground – especially by the tea ladies, who always knew I was a teetotaller. Like Jock Stein, I was always up for a cup of tea.

My relationship with managers like that was always very good, I appreciated it very much; it was very good of them to give us access to players before big games. They were never difficult to talk to, and when we talked about money for a big game we always agreed on what was a fair price; there was no haggling. I know it doesn't sound very sophisticated but that's how it was done, and we did the same when we went to Wembley, where we negotiated directly with the English FA. We once did a Scotland–England game from Wembley and ferried a film back up, processed it, edited it and showed it the same night and the rights for the game were £375 for 15 minutes of highlights from Wembley.

That was the early '60s when ITV weren't doing football and we phoned up the English FA and said, 'We know the BBC are doing it, but we would like to be involved,' and they asked how much we could afford, how much would we and where would we show it? They agreed and we filmed next to the BBC's big cameras. We did the same in Ireland at a ground which had no television platform in those days so we took four seats out of the stand and stood two cameramen side by side – a sound-recordist and me! We flew back on a charter plane at 5.30 and showed it at 10 p.m.

It was a bit daft going to Belfast with film cameras, flying the stuff back and I remember we did a real bit of showboating with a clip on the early programme as well as the 10 p.m. one. They said we'd never get it back from Belfast to Glasgow but we did a short roll in the first, about five or six minutes of the teams lining up and a bit of early play and we had a taxi which took it to the airport and a wee charter plane to Glasgow. The film arrived just after 4 p.m., they edited it and showed it at 5.05! Then the plane flew back for us and the rest of the film. Great fun.

I got a nice invitation from UEFA to go to the Champions League game last year because I had given them an interview about the 1960 European Cup, the best game any of us had ever seen, and it was great to see how these things have changed; how the press have the laptops, the television guys with their monitors . . . and their minders.

2

STARGAZING

ALEX SMITH: Billy Bremner was from the Raploch in Stirling and I was from the mining village of Cowie and when I left school at 15 I signed for a local club called Gowanhill United. That was under-21 football and one training night we had done all the training and were into the game at the end. There was an odd number, 15 of us, and this little kid was standing with a bike and his sandshoes and socks down to the ankles.

He was only 13 and a half and I told him there were grown men playing, but he came on our side and, honest to God, he was brilliant, this little red-haired lad. It told me everything about him that first night. He was so pleased at getting a game and then came and watched us for the next five or six nights. He came in the dressing-room with us and walked back from the park and Billy started playing for the team at 14. Him and me became really good friends. I would go and watch him when he got Scottish schoolboy trials and then we would go to the pictures together at night.

He was full of cheek, full of fun, full of the joys at night and loved nothing better than playing.

But again he had a humility with people. Billy saw football as the opportunity; it was a way of getting on. At 15 he was away to Leeds.

He had a nice arrogance about him that he was going to be a special footballer and never ever went on a park thinking there was someone better than him. It didn't matter if it was Pelé, Bobby Charlton or Dave Mackay. Billy was only 16 when Dave lifted him. He played in a game in the early part of his career when he was the youngest on the park at 16 and Stanley Matthews was the oldest at 49.

Billy should have been a top manager. He served his apprenticeship at Doncaster and when he went to Leeds he did very well at first. But he fell out with a director there and he lost his job.

Cheeky chappie: Billy Bremner knew he was going to be special.
(© *Daily Record*/Mirrorpix)

Sometimes when I was at Aberdeen and with Scotland Under-21, I would think: 'Why are you doing this job when someone like Billy Bremner should be doing it?'

At one Cup final, I think it was the Arsenal game, when Leeds were there he had our tickets and we missed him at the big gate. At quarter to three he comes out with all the full regalia on, boots and tracksuit, and this is 15 minutes before kick-off, and says: 'What are you worrying about?'

I said: 'Billy, this is a massive game.'

'It's just another game to be won,' he says. It was like the first game at Gowanhill Juniors, he just wasn't overawed by anything.

DAVE MACKAY: There's a famous picture of me when I was with Spurs with Billy Bremner, who was at Leeds. That match was just after I was coming back from a leg break. Everybody said, 'You've broken your leg,' but I've never broken my legs, other people broke them, and that was the first day back after two leg breaks, one after the other. Billy knew exactly which leg had been broken, and he came round behind me and the nearest leg to him was my right leg and he kicked me on the left leg. So what do you do? What would you do? I mean if he kicks me on that leg and breaks it, I'm finished, so I just grabbed him. I was so angry I could have lifted the stand. I don't think he apologised later because he was not like that. I will say he was a brilliant little player but a dirty little so-and-so. That Leeds side had a few of them and they didn't have to. Leeds United were the best team for five years but if an opposing player knocked the ball off, whack, they get it on the ankle. They wanted you to retaliate and get you sent off, which they didn't have to do as they were such a good team.

BOB CRAMPSEY: I worked for a time with probably the best penalty-taker ever, Johnny Hubbard of Rangers. He and I were in the same RAF side in England and I attribute his success to his practising on me. It was very irritating because he would wrong-foot you and the ball would always pass you not very far away and not travelling particularly quickly and it would always finish up wedged in the stanchion. He scored something like 59 out of 62, an incredible percentage. Odd that Henrik Larsson is a particularly poor penalty-taker and yet in open play he is a wonderful player. He's instinctive, hard-working, committed and very good in the air for someone who is not particularly tall.

Air commanders: Willie Bauld and Henrik Larsson had at least one thing in common: their heading ability. (both © *Daily Record*/Mirrorpix)

ERIC MILLIGAN: Willie Bauld was king of Tynecastle in those days and I was brought up to revere the name of Willie Bauld. He was at the veteran stage by then but even now when I hear that name and the others who played at Tynecastle in that era like Davie Mackay, Jimmy Murray, Jimmy Milne, Bobby Kirk and Gordon Marshall the hairs on the back of my neck start jumping a bit. Now that's irrational, but it's true. Willie was a very very good football player but to be revered by football players they have to see something of them in you and the fact that Willie had been a miner and brought up in a working-class area of Newcraighall, there was almost a sense that if he hadn't been a footballer Willie would have been stood on the terraces with a maroon scarf round his neck and getting wet when it rains. There was this sense that he was one of us. He was also a very clean player and ahead of his time in many ways because centre-forwards then were out-and-out goalscorers, but he used to play a slightly deeper position. He would also do a first-time pass without going through the business of trapping the ball and looking round for support. He was good in the air and had this ability, which Henrik Larsson has today, of holding himself in the air for that precious half-second and then heading the ball with great accuracy. But I think it was as much to do with his personality as his supreme skill.

For different reasons he never got many international caps so he was seen as first and foremost a Hearts personality, his only team, after coming here as a young boy; when he stopped playing for Hearts he stopped playing football and there was this feeling that he wasn't interested in playing for anyone else but Hearts. The Hibs had Lawrie Reilly, who was a Scottish international, so the Edinburgh teams had these two great personalities, both playing with No. 9 on their back.

Davie Mackay, who went on to Spurs, was possibly the greatest player British post-war football produced. If you were picking an all-star British post-war team you would pick Mackay and then consider who would play around him. A fantastic personality, he could do everything; he was a winner. He could tackle and pass in the same movement and another great feature of his game was his ability to take throw-ins because he could take a throw and reach the far post, like he was taking a corner.

FORDYCE MAXWELL: Certain players stick in your mind. In the late '50s, early '60s they had a goalkeeper called Tommy McQueen who was Gordon McQueen's dad and he was an absolute character along with a full-back called Charlie Beacham and a big centre-half called John Rugg. One of the things I remember was Charlie scoring an own goal and Tommy chasing him up the pitch. Rugg was a good centre-half and a very good penalty-taker. He would run up as if he was going to take it with his right foot and then take it with his left, which was quite a clever thing to do. Tommy was a well-known pigeon fancier locally and used to do well in races. They were local lads and you would see them wandering round town. Fans tend to think about the team rather than players at Berwick's level and the players we have had were mainly a lot of honest triers. Tommy Craig, a winger, was very popular with the fans and I would be interested to see any film of John Rugg. He really was a very good centre-half.

Jock Wallace was there for a time, a top player playing out his career. The rest were part-timers. There was a chap called Ken Bowron, a local school teacher, who banged in a lot of goals in the early to mid-'60s. Full-back Gordon Haig played there for a long time and it is these guys who have shown the kind of loyalty the fans tend to remember most. You identify with them.

ERIC MILLIGAN: Three football players were brought up within a stone's throw of each other in Gorgie: Davie Mackay, Graeme Souness – another lionheart – and the same community that spawned these two also spawned, between the two, Willie Jardine, who Rangers supporters always refer to as Sandy Jardine for some reason. He was at Tynecastle School with me and was a fantastic young football player.

People in Scotland talk of the dominance of the Glasgow clubs, but most of the greatest players at Rangers have had Edinburgh associations. Willie Jardine, Ralph Brand, Jimmy Miller, John Greig, Willie Woodburn and Souness in more recent times. I just wish all those players had devloped their careers at Easter Road or Tynecastle.

PETER DONALD: I personally believe that in his time Danny McGrain was the best full-back in the world. It's rare that you can say that Scotland has the best player in the world in any specific position but in my view when Danny was on top form he was incredible – he was the best in the world in that position. He had such character. He didn't have everything because he couldn't score a goal. In fact, I was at Celtic Park for a Scottish Cup tie many, many years ago – I think it was Queen of the South they were playing – and I was sitting in the directors' box beside Sir Robert Kelly's wife Lady Kelly and Danny was doing his wee run up the park and he actually scored. Now the reaction of the fans, of everybody, was to laugh. Not because they were laughing at him, but because they were just so happy he had scored. They were used to Danny doing everything else but not scoring, and here he scored. And I said quite casually: 'Aye, it's been a while since Danny McGrain scored,' and Lady Kelly turned round just like that and gave me exactly the last time that he had scored – she knew to a T. She was a fan.

BOB CRAMPSEY: I once asked Bobby Charlton and Paddy Crerand the same question: who in the Leeds United side were you afraid of? They both said John Giles. Come on, I said, we are talking Jack Charlton; we are talking Norman Hunter. Paddy said: 'No, you could go and have a cup of tea in the time they took to tackle and you always saw them coming. With Giles the ball would always be around and you could never be sure if he was going for the ball or you, nor could the referee.'

PETER DONALD: I think that these type of guys were the top of their tree, Souness in his heyday was a great player and in Italy he lifted himself from being an ordinary player. He had an aura and presence about him. When he came back from Italy everybody thought that if he were a piece of chocolate he would eat himself, but he had a presence and Jock Stein used that when he was his manager. Then there are the Alan Roughs of this world – relaxed, pleasant people, who are good fun to travel with. Some players have got a reputation but they are actually good human beings. Andy Goram is a classic example, a daft laddie now and again, his own worst enemy, but great fun. In hotel corridors all throughout the world players are players and some would walk past you with their heads down and just ignore you, but never Andy. If he saw you in the street he would cross the street to you. It is his personality that makes him a good guy, not being a footballer.

DAVID MOYES: When I was younger, Jimmy Johnstone and Willie Henderson were the ones you were always trying to be in the park or in the street in Glasgow. They were the typical Scottish player, dribblers – exciting to watch. Scotland have always had great players playing down here in England; every manager wanted a Scot in the team. A man with fire in the belly and who was sharp with their wit, and good about the place. Recently it has turned so there's not as many players but fortunately the managers from Scotland have been relatively successful over the last few years.

My favourite player has to be Danny McGrain. Michel Platini and Maradona were fantastic players, but you move on all the time. You look at them, and people like Zidane, and think why, and how, and wonder if there are any more like them out there that we can get!

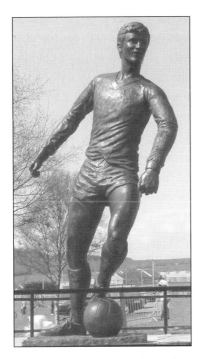

In loving memory: Jim Baxter's statue in his home town of Hill o'Beith. Fans raised £60,000 to build it.
(Photo courtesy of Raith Rovers FC)

GORDON BROWN: A few weeks ago I had the great privilege, with his mother, of unveiling the Jim Baxter statue in Hill o'Beith in Fife. Alex Ferguson was president of the appeal that raised some £60,000 for this statue in his home village. Baxter was my hero at Raith Rovers and he was a great player; even if he did believe training was for other people. He was a great character too, and a very nice guy. I remember speaking at the function where he was named midfield player of the century for Scotland. This was the night when they had Bobby Charlton there and Bobby Robson, who had both come up for this presentation, and all evening they replayed all the Scotland goals and never played one England goal!

I mentioned that Baxter had been sold from Raith Rovers to Rangers for £16,500 and he corrected me and said it was £17,500. And I told him: 'Well, I think Raith Rovers only got £16,500!'

In 1967, he told me, he had

Jim Baxter with Billy Bremner.
(© *Daily Record*/Mirrorpix)

111

kept running back into the defence and telling them to get up the field because they would never have a better chance of scoring a goal against England at Wembley. Baxter shone alongside Willie McNaught at Raith Rovers, who was a great centre-half. It was a good team at that time but he was always going to go further. The great tragedy, of course, is that Baxter's career was over before he was 30.

ERIC MILLIGAN: The first time I went through to Hampden for the Scotland–England game was in 1960 when Joe Baker, the Hibs centre-forward, was playing for England against Scotland. Alex Young, the Hearts centre-forward, played inside-right for Scotland because Ian St John played centre-forward and John Cumming, the Hearts captain, played wing-half that day and the reason he played was because Tottenham would not release Davie Mackay. We have come a long way since those days. They got a draw with a Bobby Charlton penalty and I can remember being a bit unhappy, not least because Joe Baker of Hibs was playing for England. Why, when he was brought up in Wishaw?

ALEX TOTTEN: I played against George Best early on and even then his talent was outstanding. Tommy McLean gave you a hard time, Willie Henderson, Jimmy Johnstone, but when wee Jimmy beat you, you always got a second chance because he would want to beat you, again. Willie would just put the ball past you and you would never see him again.

BOB CRAMPSEY: I was a goalkeeper and Queen's Park had an Egyptian keeper just before the war called Mustafa Mansour, who finished up as minister for tourism in Egypt. He died not so long ago. He was a very, in the strict sense of the word, exotic goalkeeper. He was very lithe and caused all sorts of uproar at Hampden by punching the ball clear. It was interesting that the ones in the crowd bawling at him for failing to clutch the ball were not the ones receiving a 12-stone centre-forward at the same time.

ARTHUR MONTFORD: I tended to enjoy the skilful players, players who could do things with the ball. Jimmy Mason of the now defunct Third Lanark was a lovely, gifted old-fashioned inside-forward.

Skill and bite: Rangers captain John Greig. (© *Daily Record*/Mirrorpix)

The Rangers side that won the Cup-Winners' Cup captained by John Greig was a good side; it had skill as well as bite and you could say the same for the Lisbon Lions. I also have a soft spot for goalkeepers. We did a wonderful feature with the Kilmarnock goalie Jocky Robertson about why penalties are missed, and a guy wrote in to *Scotsport* and said, 'I can guarantee to score from every penalty kick.' So I went back and I said: 'Well, I'll set it up for you and you come in and do it.' So he came in and he had this theory of his own about how to score them. But I said to him: 'You haven't worked out why people miss them,' and he said: 'It's because people don't pick the right angle,' and I said: 'No, no, it's because of what happens up here.' The closer it got to taking them the tenser he got. I promised him I would leave the camera running, not cut it or edit it and we ran and he scored four out of ten. Jocky saved a couple and the rest just went over the post or hit the bar.

TERRY CHRISTIE: I was at Dundee in the halcyon days when they won the League. They had a great team in 1961 and it was maybe the happiest time of my life rubbing shoulders with these great players like Gordon Smith and Alan Gilzean. I was an outside-right and was supposed to be under-studying Gordon Smith, but the manager, Bob Shankly, had a few in his mind to put in the team before me. Post-war with Hibs, Gordon was the David Beckham of his time. He did this thing that every year he went abroad for his holidays and came back a bronzed hero and the women idolised him. He was tall, he was handsome, and played football like you cannot believe it and even as a 39-year-old in the Dundee team he was wonderful.

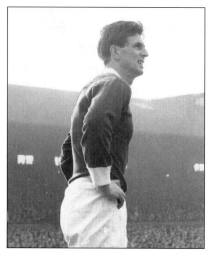

Greatest of them all? Gordon Smith of Hibs, Hearts, Dundee and Scotland. (© The Scotsman Publications Limited)

LORD MACFARLANE: My all-time favourite was Gordon Smith. I thought he was really an astounding player. He certainly, like so many other players at that time, was never at his best in international matches, but to see Gordon Smith playing well for his club in that astonishing forward line was really something memorable. I used to love Willie Waddell, funnily enough another outside-right, running down the wing to the corner flag and stopping and crossing for Willie Thornton to head a goal; absolutely classic Scottish football. We've had some great players. I'm a great admirer of Kenny Dalglish, a hugely interesting footballer, in the sense that he was relatively small but he had this marvellous ability to keep the ball close and shield the ball with his body as though he was 6ft 6in. and 15 stone. A great gift. Watching a footballer with brains is a great delight and it's not too difficult to recognise one.

JOHN HUGHES: When I was at Berwick I played with Ralph Callaghan and Ralph is still one of the best players I've ever played with. He never said too much to you, just went about his business and you could see Jim Jefferies blasting him in at half-time and Ralph wouldn't respond. Ralph just used to say: 'Well, I'll just knock it up to you, you just use your strength, hold it, and I'll come in for the return.'

BOB CRAMPSEY: The best player I've ever seen was Stanley Matthews. I saw Finney and Matthews every week for about two years and I thought Finney was a hell of a good player, but I think Matthews had reached a point where he thought the scoring of goals was for the artisans. The game was about the creation of goals. I was raving away about Matthews to Stanley Mortensen once about the 1953 Cup final, the so-called Matthews final, and he turned to me and said: 'You know, I got a hat-trick in that match!'

Matthews was the exact antithesis of Didier Agathe. They could both run the length of the field and get to the line, the difference was what happened when they got there. Matthews was extraordinary because he never appeared to be moving at all and it was only when you saw the left-back who was toiling and toiling away in his wake . . .

DAVID MOYES: I had become coach then assistant manager while still playing. Management was something I wanted to do, and was a natural progression. I carried on in the Preston reserves when I was manager until I decided I couldn't stand in the way of young kids coming through. I had lots of help. The president at Preston, Sir Tom Finney, is a great man, he always used to come and see me on Fridays before a match and he wasn't the old player telling you what it was like in his day. He was up to date and precise and supportive and you could not meet a better man in football. A gentleman. I never saw him play, but people say he was a fantastic player with great ability . . . but, more importantly, great humility.

LAWRIE REILLY: David Beckham would find it difficult bending one of those old leather balls and as far as I am concerned when you look at Tom Finney, Stanley Matthews and Gordon Smith in Scotland, he is not one iota better than these three.

DAVID McGREGOR: Famous Forfar players. Archie Knox played as a very young schoolboy for Forfar West End Juniors and came to Forfar in '65 and it's still the second result he looks for every week. He still keeps in touch with myself and one or two others and we had a drink with him before the Champions League game at Old Trafford. John Clark is still playing for an amateur team in the town at the age of 46 or whatever. Dave McQueen, who was an immortal of Scottish football just before and after the Great War, and one of the few people who played for both Rangers and Celtic, was Forfar born and bred and had a senior career spanning something like 32 years – which would be unheard of in this day and age. Craig Brewster began his senior career with us and he is another who has a great affection for the club, as are Stewart Petrie, who went to Dunfermline and is now in Australia, and Ian McPhee, who ended up playing nearly 600 games for the club in two spells.

CRAIG LEVEIN: I have great memories of the Hearts team I played in, but John Robertson achieved something huge when he beat the club goal-scoring record. I played against a lot of good guys. A lot of them came up here once Souness arrived, like Terry Butcher, Mark Hateley and Maurice Johnston. My favourite player when I was growing up was Alan Hansen. I like centre-backs who can play good football, although I don't like them as much as a manager. I told my mum at four or five years old that I was going to be a professional footballer and I did; it was something that I set as the prime goal of my life and it always was. Now it's something I've managed to achieve, and once achieved it has now paid me back by giving me the opportunity to be a coach and to stay in the game. This game is just part of my life and I don't envisage myself at some point down the line deciding I've had enough of this. I still find it a challenge and new things happen every day. There are new characters who will walk into your dressing-room every year and things are continually changing so it doesn't get stale.

DAVID McGREGOR: Back in the mid-'60s we actually had a Brazilian playing for us for about four or five weeks. I'm not quite sure where he came from, but he stayed with the Forfar club secretary at the time, Jim Robertson, who was in the job even longer than I've been now. Jim was a bachelor and I always mind Jim said he got rid of the player because he couldn't keep him in bananas. I think Jim was trying to feed him on Forfar bridies and mince and tatties, which was a bit alien to a young Brazilian, so he decided just to try and live on bananas, and Jim couldn't keep up the supply.

IAN BLACK: My boyhood hero was a chap called Peter Dickson, who we signed from Albion Rovers in 1975. He scored a goal or two every game and he saved us from relegation. We used to sing a song 'Peter Dickson Walks on Water'. He was God basically. That same season we played Ayr United in the Scottish Cup; we drew 2–2 up at Ayr and the replay at Palmerston we beat them 5–4 after extra-time, with Dickson scoring the winner, and that always will be one of the best games I ever remember. The draw had taken place on the Saturday night and the replay was on the Wednesday so we knew who we were going to get in the next round, Rangers. We played Rangers that season twice. We played them in the League Cup and then in the Scottish Cup and they beat us 5–0 – they had Davie Cooper, Mark Hateley, John Greig and Peter McCloy.

GORDON SHERRY: Ray Montgomerie was a great Kilmarnock captain and he is still involved there. Paul Wright seemed to fritter away but he was good for Killie and latterly Ian Durrant, who was just incredible, a player with superb vision. I've played a lot of golf with Alex Totten and I know Bobby Williamson really well. He will often text me asking if I want tickets for a match.

Nowadays, of course, I wind him up if Kilmarnock beat Hibs.

I used to go up to Glenbervie or Gleneagles to play with Alex and I very rarely beat him because I was giving him too many shots. He played off 12 and when I was an amateur I was plus 4. Then I turned pro and we kept the games going and I told him: 'Four less shots now, Alex.' I would still just about manage a half. We would play for a small wager, an undisclosed fee as they would say. A few footballers are keen on golf. Gordon Marshall was a very good player, as was Gus McPherson – I was very friendly with him. Gus played off two or three and is now assistant manager at St Mirren.

JIM LEISHMAN: Heroes. Alex Smith was a hero, Alex Ferguson was a hero, Bert Paton and Charlie Dixon who is a folk hero at Dunfermline for scoring the goals in the Cup. These were the guys I was looking up to as a kid; I used to read about them in the papers and then there I was playing with them. Brilliant.

As a defender Roy Barrie was my idol because he was a tough defender and that's how I used to look on myself. I think I was on an upward trend when I broke my leg at 20. Jim Jefferies was involved in that and it's still a bit of a sore point. The injury was horrific, a terrible injury. I have scars from the injury and the operations, and I knew after 15 months I was never going to get back to the standard of before. When it happened I was in the old First Division and when I went back they were in the bottom division and if I couldn't work it in the bottom division, I was never going to get anywhere. That was the time I started looking at a full-time job and becoming a part-time player, and that was when I became involved in the coaching side.

IAN WILSON: I must have played around 400 games for Leicester when they had Tommy Williams and John O'Neill in defence and Eddie Kelly in midfield. Alan Smith and Gary Lineker were around and I still stay in touch with them. Gary was a young boy who had come through the youth team and they stuck him in the reserves, at outside-right. I was coming back from injury at the time and Jock phoned me later and asked how Lineker had played. I said he was like lightning but he always used to fall on his backside when he was playing out there. He was great to play with. If you were in trouble as a midfield player and you knocked it over the defence Gary would get on to it with his pace even if it wasn't directly in his path; he'd turn a poor pass into a good one. He is a lovely fellow and very intelligent and great at quizzes! He'd tell you certain things about champions in sports and you'd hardly have heard of the sport. We were a bit of a bogey team for Liverpool in those days. Anfield was a wonderful place to play, a great playing surface and fans who appreciate you. We usually beat them there and did the double over them in our first year back in First Division. We beat them 2–0 at Filbert Street and 2–1 at their place and Alan Younger scored an own goal – so we scored all five goals in the two meetings.

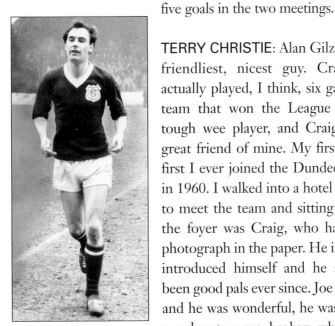

Shrewd operator: Alan Gilzean became a folk hero at Dens Park and White Hart Lane.
(© *Daily Record*/Mirrorpix)

TERRY CHRISTIE: Alan Gilzean was the friendliest, nicest guy. Craig Brown actually played, I think, six games in the team that won the League and was a tough wee player, and Craig became a great friend of mine. My first game, the first I ever joined the Dundee party, was in 1960. I walked into a hotel in Glasgow to meet the team and sitting in there in the foyer was Craig, who had seen my photograph in the paper. He immediately introduced himself and he and I have been good pals ever since. Joe Baker came and he was wonderful, he was a star, and our hearts were broken when Joe got transferred to Torino, it was a sad day in the Christie household. Joe's dad was in the Army at Aldershot, so Joe Baker was born in England and played for England. For one international he got the train from Scotland, got off at King's Cross and hailed a taxi to take him to the England training headquarters and when the taxi man heard the Scots accent he said, 'Who are you kidding, son?' Joe's good at that story.

DAVE MACKAY: My heroes at Hearts were Alfie Conn, Willie Bauld. Alex Young was younger than me, but he was one of my heroes because he could play. John White was brilliant, a lovely balanced player like your Cliff Jones or Jimmy Greaves; so composed as well. John was much stronger than he looked, a strong lad. Alan Gilzean, him and Greavesie were a perfect double act. Gilly used to get up and flick it on with his head and on the end of it every time whether he headed it to the left or to the right, was Greavesie.

CHARLIE REID: The players I admired in the '70s in terms of football quality were the likes of Pat Stanton, Alex Cropley and Alex Edwards; Billy Bremner for his tenacity and toughness; Kenny Dalglish could have played for any team in the world and Jimmy Johnstone was an utterly, utterly brilliant player.

In the modern day, Franck Sauzee without any doubt. So few people remember, not just the skill, but the immense bravery of Sauzee. There was a tight Hearts game when we won 3–1 in the end and Sauzee scored a goal with a looping header, right over the top. Just as he got to the ball Gary Naysmith, totally by accident, brought his head back and

French without tears: Franck Sauzee pulled the strings for Hibs. (© *Daily Record*/Mirrorpix)

smashed into Franck's face. He lost three teeth and he just got up and carried on. People say: 'Oh aye, the Scottish players and the British players are much tougher and these Gallic players are just softies.' But how many Scottish players would get up and play on after losing three teeth? Real guts, real skill.

I have to say, Hibs got very lucky; they signed Sauzee and they signed Russell Latapy. The best thing that ever happened with Franck was when he had to move back to sweeper because when he did that he found his greatest role. Although Hibs maybe didn't get the best of him in terms of his fitness, in the role of sweeper he was absolutely fantastic.

I definitely get starstruck. I met Gordon Smith very briefly, just to shake his hand, and I must admit I was awestruck. The same with Lawrie Reilly and Joe Baker, the guys my dad used to talk about. Any of those guys who saw Gordon at his peak all agree about his greatness. My dad also spoke of Willie Bauld of Hearts and my dad played against Dave Mackay early on and recalled how hard he was to play against even then.

JOHN HUGHES: Simon Stainrod was at Falkirk and he's a great guy, the most confident guy I've ever met. He's got that swagger and when you mix that swagger from Sheffield with a guy from Leith with a crew cut there's a collision and the two of us were hammer and tongs at each other, but all in good spirits. We used to start fisticuffs, just body-shots, and everybody used to stand on the benches and me and him would get battered into each other. Many a time I've come back and had a wee crack in my hand from punching him. Oooh, the two of us got on like a house on fire, really. All my friends in football are from my Falkirk days – Brian Rice, Ian McCall, Eddie Main, Neil Oliver who I played with at Falkirk. I first met Neil Oliver at Berwick and when I got sold to Swansea he got sold to Blackburn Rovers and when I got brought back to Falkirk he brought Neil from Blackburn Rovers back to Falkirk and he's godfather to one of my twins along with Ian McCall.

Star pupil: Kenny Miller went from Musselburgh Grammar to Easter Road and Molineux. (© The Scotsman Publications Limited)

TERRY CHRISTIE: My last day at Stenhousemuir, we played Rangers in the Scottish Cup and that's a really good story. One of my pupils at Musselburgh Grammar School was a young lad called Kenny Miller. I knew his dad Jocky very well and he was a good junior player. Kenny was a lovely lad in school, never a minute's bother, and Kenny was with the Hibs. I used to watch him on a Saturday morning playing, and I remember once I pulled him into the office and gave him a tip here and there. He was so embarrassed, his head teacher bringing him into the headmaster's room and giving him a tip on how to play football. So Kenny was with the Hibs and you know he was standing still a bit. I think he had one or two games, so I phoned Alex McLeish and asked for him on loan. So we took him on loan and he did great things but he was keen to play in the Scottish Cup and they wouldn't allow us to get him Cup-tied because he was still playing for Hibs. So in the Cup we played Whitehill Welfare at Whitehill and we only drew without Kenny. In the meantime they made the draw for the next round and we were drawn against Rangers!

I had a hell of a time persuading Rod Petrie to give us permission to play Kenny, and Rod being a keen counter of pennies and pounds we had to give Hibs a considerable amount of money to get their permission to allow us to play Kenny. And, of course, we beat Whitehill 2–1 and who scored the two goals? Kenny Miller.

DAVE MACKAY: Everybody says to me, 'Who is the best player?' and I could say, 'Well, I could give you a team.' I think one particular guy is John Charles. When I was at Tottenham he played for Juventus in Italy and he was playing centre-forward and when he had left Leeds he was playing centre-half and he was just as good at centre-forward as he was at centre-half. He was an immense lad, his build was fantastic, his height was tremendous and if that was my body then I would be a better player than I ever was. He was a brilliant player.

JOHN HUGHES: I stayed in the Celtic team all the 1995–96 season and I played alongside Paolo Di Canio, John Collins – all these guys – Tom Boyd, Peter Grant, Jackie McNamara, Tosh McKinlay, big Gordon Marshall and all these guys. It was a great year. We were unlucky we never won anything, but we really played some great football and obviously the highlight of that was when I scored at Ibrox in the Old Firm game, a 1–1 draw.

TERRY CHRISTIE: The best player I have actually signed is Darren Jackson, who I signed for Meadowbank as a young skinny, wee boy. The best player that I coached was John Robertson who was a pupil of mine at Portobello High School and the best player that I've actually rubbed shoulders with was Alan Gilzean because Gordon Smith was past his best. I played with Gilly in a reserve match once down at Kilmarnock when he was coming back from injury and Tottenham Hotspur had all the scouts watching him. I was outside-right and of course he's used to Gordon Smith playing down the right and sending over crosses that he would just nod into the net. My crosses were going everywhere and I remember him absolutely shouting to me, 'Terry you'll have me playing in the Highland League.' Talk about pressure!

DOUGRAY SCOTT: The players I looked up to at Hibs were John Brownlie and Pat Stanton. Both of them were phenomenal players. I met John Brownlie recently. I was on Richard and Judy being interviewed and they gave me a football jersey, the new Hibs strip, and John Brownlie came on to present it to me. I was more starstruck than him. He was 19, I think, when he signed for Hibs and he was the original wing-back.

Pat Stanton was the governor, just one of the best midfield players I've ever seen. He really bossed the midfield and everyone was really disappointed when he moved to Celtic. I think he's kind of reappeared at Easter Road – he goes to all the games. A lovely man.

JOHN HUGHES: Some of the Celtic players were on mega wages but that has never really bothered me. Tommy Burns respected the job I did for Celtic as a centre-half and I used to say, 'Well, I'm just a guy who's making my way through the game and I may be a good honest tradesman at times.' But I gave it everything I had, which was appreciated by the Celtic fans, who took to me. They knew my style, which was that nothing got left out on the park and I never let them down, never ever let them down.

DOUGRAY SCOTT: Joe Jordan and Gordon McQueen were good players, Jimmy Johnstone was a great player and Dave Narey scored that fantastic goal against Brazil when we got beat 4–1. Jimmy Hill said it was a toe-poke. I admire a good defender. John Blackley was a great defender, big Jim Black as well, but I mean midfielders are always the ones that catch my eye just

The governor: Pat Stanton's star quality made its mark on a young Dougray Scott.
(© *Daily Record*/Mirrorpix)

because I played in midfield too, I suppose, but someone who has a bit of creativity, and someone who's got passing the ball, for me a bit of an all rounder. Pat Stanton was that kind of man, he was a good tackler, a good distributor, someone who's got great vision. Willie Johnstone was a great player for us as well.

ALLAN GRIEVE: At Stirling, we've not had many players who've gone on to play really at the very highest level. John

John Colquhoun of Hearts shoots to score against Celtic, season 1985–86.
(© *Daily Record*/Mirrorpix)

Colquhoun, who played for us in the early '80s, was an outstanding striker and went on to play for Celtic and Hearts, and had a wee spell in England with Sunderland and Millwall. He got a Scotland cap, and he was one of the best players who we've brought on. One who we introduced this season, a young goalkeeper, Ian Turner, played for us at the start of the season just past, 2002–03. He is an outstanding goalkeeper and we sold him to Everton at Christmas for £50,000. He's the best young goalkeeper I've ever seen and I'm sure he'll make the grade with Everton and end up as an international goalkeeper. And he's from Stirling. We've had a lot of good goalkeepers, but we're one of these teams where goalkeepers seem to stay a long time. The time thing I've been watching, there's really only been half a dozen Albion goalkeepers and all have played 300 or 400 games, but Ian Turner is as good, in fact better, than any of them I've seen.

BRIAN FLYNN: My first Scotland international was '73 when we beat the then Czechoslovakia. Joe Jordan scored with a diving header and I remember on the old shale terracing at Hampden the dust would have choked you to death after the reaction raised by that goal.

These were the golden years for Scottish players as far as I'm concerned, players like Davie Cooper, Kenny Dalglish, Joe Jordan, Gordon McQueen, Alan Hansen, Danny McGrain – great, fantastic players, but you have to ask 'Where are they now?' You've got to ask yourself the question, 'Why are we not producing them?' It has to be

Pride of Scotland: Kenny Dalglish.
(© *Daily Record*/Mirrorpix)

said that the kids aren't playing in the street any longer but neither are Dutch kids or German kids. The African and South American countries are flourishing because kids are kicking a ball down the street before they get into youth club teams. Then they play for school, are naturally fit and they go out in the evening, and that's all they do.

ALEX McLEISH: My philosophy has always been to take one step at a time – if you aim too high you can be disappointed. I had to make sure I grafted. I wasn't gifted in the way that Gordon Strachan or Dalglish were and I knew that anything I was going to get out of the game I was going to have to work for. If I could pass one message on to kids now it would be that whatever they do, whether it's football or education, they give it everything they can.

At Aberdeen we had players there already like Willie Miller, Stuart Kennedy from Falkirk, who came as an incredibly speedy full-back and with a massive will to win, Gordon Strachan, Mark McGhee. They all had fantastic appetites to win football matches. In charge we had Ally McLeod who had a fantastic bubbly personality and then Billy McNeill took it on a bit. He had great knowledge, being a European Cup winner, and he brought a lot to the club and not least to me. He helped me with the technical side of centre-half play.

When Alex Ferguson arrived he inherited all these guys who wanted to win. His leadership qualities added to what was there already plus bringing some shrewd acquisitions of his own turned us into the great force we became.

RICHARD GORDON: I would have been at various matches in 1969, but it's 1970 that I really remember and that was the team that won the Scottish Cup. So they were middling away in the league but set off on this Cup run and I guess my initial heroes were Bobby Clark, the goalkeeper who was an Aberdeen stalwart for many years, and Joe Harper, who was the main goalscorer. The other one was Arthur Graham, who was at the time 17, a young left-winger, signed from Cambuslang Rangers. Arthur was just emerging and I always remember the thrill of seeing his No. 11 shirt going down the wing, that and the fact that he was a boy only seven years older than I was, and he was playing for the team I loved. During that Cup run, we played a semi-final against Kilmarnock at Muirton Park and Derek Mackay scored the only goal. I was at both of those games and so suddenly for me a new hero emerged.

King Arthur: Aberdeen found a star at Cambuslang in Arthur Graham. (Photo courtesy of Aberdeen FC)

JULIE FLEETING: In San Diego there is a squad of 20 and they look after us really well. There are four foreign players allowed in a team and apart from me one's from China, one is from Canada and one is from Brazil. At first it was a bit of a shock for my friends and family – a 22-year-old girl from Ayrshire playing professional football in America – but now they love to hear how I'm getting on and they're always asking. There is a lot of competition for first-team places and even though I captain Scotland I'm always fighting for a start. I miss games because I'm playing for Scotland, so when I go back I'm not going to be an automatic choice. In the States the tempo there is much higher and there is a bigger emphasis on getting in the gym for weight training. The pluses are the big crowds and the sun and it's great to get paid for doing something I love. There is a real family atmosphere at games, maybe like it was in Scotland at one time. In the current Scotland squad I think Barry Ferguson is one that

ALLOA FOOTBALL &
ATHLETIC CLUB, LTD.

RECREATION GROUNDS

REGISTERED OFFICE: 41 MILL STREET.

41 Mill Street,

Alloa. 8th.September 1939.

Mr. Alex Yatt
Kincardine

Dear *Alex* Sir,   The War and Football.

        The following decisions were made at a Special Meeting of
the Scottish Football Association held on 6th.inst.
1. In conformity with the Government order,all football in Scotland
   shall be suspended until further notice.
2. The registrations of the players with the Association shall remain
   effective meantime. (Players are debarred from playing for any
   Club other than that for whom they are so registered)
3. All contracts or agreements between clubs and players shall be
   suspended as from 3rd.September -the date of the Government's
   decree.

        The Directors very much regret in the circumstances having to
suspend your contract until further notice and sincerely trust it
will not be long before you will be recalled to commence playing
again.

        Expenses due are enclosed for which kindly acknowledge
receipt.

                        Yours faithfully,
                        Geo R Mathewson
                            Secretary.

P.S. In order that same may be stored away at the Ground kindly
     return boots and spikes recently purchased.Postage will be
     refunded.

Game off: Even the power of the SFA could not halt the suspension of all
football in September 1939, as this letter from Alloa FC to its players illustrates.
(courtesy of Alloa FC)

The way we were:
Cathkin Park, once
home of Third Lanark;
and a modern
equivalent, Stark's Park,
Kirkcaldy (below).
(© *Daily
Record*/Mirrorpix)
(courtesy of Raith
Rovers FC)

Tynecastle greats: Willie Bauld on a training run while Dave Mackay shows off his cultured left foot. (both © *Daily Record*/Mirrorpix)

Shankly's boys: Dundee with the 1961–62 Championship trophy. Back row, left to right: Pat Liney, Gordon Smith, Alan Gilzean, Bobby Wishart, Ian Ure, Bob Shankly and Bobby Seith. Front row, left to right: Andy Penman, Bobby Cox, Alex Hamilton, Alan Cousin and Hugh Robertson. (© *Daily Record*/Mirrorpix)

Super fans: Scottish football has earned faithful support from all walks of life. Top left, Lord Macfarlane; top right left, Brian Flynn; below left, top golfer Gordon Sherry and below right, The Proclaimers – Craig and Charlie Reid – with John Collins.
(all © *Daily Record*/Mirrorpix)

Sport and politics: They do mix, in the cases of first minister Jack McConnell, (left) and sports minister Frank McAveety (below). (©SNS Group) (© *Daily Record*/Mirrorpix)

In the hot seat: Scottish football has long boasted great characters among its managers; oppostie, John Lambie, Terry 'The Duffle' Christie and Paul Sturrock; this page: Jim Leishman, Alex McLeish in his Motherwell days and a kilted Alex Totten. (all © *Daily Record*/Mirrorpix)

Eurocrats: AC Milan skipper Paolo Maldini, referee Willie Young and Rangers captain Barry Ferguson with friends line up at Ibrox for a pre-season friendly in July 2002. (courtesy of Willie Young)

Fanatical about football: The Tartan Army have proved themselves the greatest supporters on the planet. (© SNS Group)

stands out for anyone who's been watching internationals. I suppose I'm a bit like him when I'm playing for Scotland. I'm not a noisy captain – I don't shout and scream at them – I'm more the quiet kind and just try and lead.

JOHN HUGHES: In the football environment everybody mucks in together, even at somewhere like Celtic. It's all hands on deck and that was the philosophy there. If you are gonna go out and somebody's flinging the kitchen sink at you like at Ibrox and you're gonna buckle, you're no good to me. That got instilled in me at Falkirk with Jim Jefferies and I saw it at Celtic even more. We used to go into Celtic at 9 a.m. and by quarter past you wouldn't get a seat in the dressing-room, and we didn't start training until the back of 10. You wouldn't get a mat in the gymnasium, everybody would be in doing their stomachs, their press-ups and speed ball.

PETER DONALD: When you travel with the international team as an administrator you're a necessary evil to some degree. There's quite a distinct line of control; the coaches look after the players, the administrators look after the combination of officials and make sure they get to the places they are supposed to be going and all that sort of stuff. Players are generally easy to deal with.

In the '70s and '80s they weren't huge superstars but they were still big stars. The players recognised that you were in charge of their expenses and were usually very kind to you, and you never had any problems. I used to have many discussions with Kenny Dalglish about his expenses, but it's a very relaxed relationship and again it's the view of the outside world, that the international footballer has an exciting life, travelling here and there to exotic places, but the reality is that they come off the plane, onto buses, into hotels and then are training, sleeping, playing then reversing the whole process and heading back home. There's no element of being a tourist – these are workers going to their business and doing their job.

JOHN HUGHES: I enjoyed playing with Paul McStay at Celtic. I thought he was a genius, with feet like Fred Astaire. You could give him a ball in the phone box and you wouldn't get it off him. I know everybody says he could have scored more goals and he could have done this or that, but Paul, he was the band leader, he orchestrated everything. What a football player; he was absolutely fantastic. You had the craft of Di Canio and then you had your Sauzees and your Latapys and right back to my Falkirk days, Maurice Johnston.

No one knows what a professional Maurice was or what a trainer. He would train all day if you asked him, and he had the attributes.

ALLAN GRIEVE: I've watched hundreds and hundreds of games other than Stirling Albion matches, you know. I go to a lot of midweek games involving other clubs, internationals, European games and so on and probably the best player I've seen would have been Kenny Dalglish in his prime playing for Celtic, Scotland and Liverpool. He was absolutely brilliant. He played against us in a couple of Cup ties in the early '70s and he is the best player that I've ever seen. The most impressive thing to me was his temperament in that he seldom lost his head, even in high pressure Rangers v. Celtic games. He was able to just keep his cool, keep above the hurly burly of it. I think that he had the ability just to be in the right place and find the right space. I enjoyed watching him, also really enjoyed watching Dundee United's teams in the '80s, that did so well in Europe. I thought guys like Paul Sturrock, Davy Narey and so on were fantastic players and Dundee United were totally overachieving at that time. They reached the UEFA Cup final and a European Cup semi-final, so a team like that was just phenomenal and it's interesting that the vast majority of them were from Dundee and the surrounding area – local guys who had come through the system at Tannadice.

STUART COSGROVE: Paul Sturrock. We certainly like our lugs in Perth because we also had Billy Dodds for a time. Paul is still called Judas by some fanzines because he went to Dundee United and he was a United fan, but there's a part of me that can forgive him that. There are people who get fundamentalist about this. Paul is from Pitlochry, which is in Perthshire, but geographically he is as close to Tannadice as Perth. He was a great junior player at Pitlochry and when he got signed for Dundee United he went straight into the team – United's greatest ever. My cousin Ross was a centre-half and he played for Arbroath and one day Arbroath were asked to go and play at Tannadice in a closed-doors game before one of their European games to get Sturrock fit again to play Barcelona. Ross to this day swears it was the biggest nightmare of his life. Ross said he had fantasised that day he was a senior footballer and that day he realised the gap between where he was and where this guy was. Sure enough, off Sturrock went and put a few past Barcelona.

Paul is manager down in Plymouth. My job takes me down there and when I'm there I'm always swotting up the local papers to find out about Luggy and Plymouth as he took a few Scottish players down there.

JACK McCONNELL: I had a mixed bag of players I liked watching. The players who appealed to me were Joe Jordan and Andy Gray and I liked the idea that you had centre-forwards who were fearless and would go anywhere. The games they played in were never boring and they were my heroes as a teenager. I followed Leeds United a lot, for some reason, and supported them through the '70s, and they had a big Scottish presence: Bremner, Gray and Lorimer with the fantastic shot.

BRIAN FLYNN: Bobby Cunningham and John Prentice were here when football managers had respect and the players had respect. I met some players and they were just ordinary guys and I couldn't understand this; this was a football player, you know, I thought there would be something different about them. There's a guy called George Gibson who played centre-half and he was just absolutely magnificent. I remember him just strolling through and spraying passes, and I just thought, 'That's who I want to be.'

HUGH WALLACE: Last year we had a player on loan from Kilmarnock who was actually the assistant groundsman at Rugby Park and for some games he wasn't available because he was needed at Rugby Park. Sometimes players couldn't come to matches because they were home babysitting and the wife was out working. When I was younger, Willie Henderson of Rangers was my favourite player. My mother always thought I was going to be inviting him home for tea one day. She thought he lived with us because I spoke about him so much. He was the entertainer and that is what fans look for. Denis Law, too, although I remember a Scotland v. Austria game at Hampden when the referee abandoned the game because he had sent off so many Austrians, which may have had something to do with Denis! Bobby Charlton was also a favourite, one of few Englishmen respected up here; Bobby Moore, too, when he stopped playing.

JACK McCONNELL: I won't name names for fear of embarrassing them, but whenever I meet international football stars I am like any other fan. Starstruck. They will say: 'Oh, it's very nice to meet you, First Minister,' and I will say, 'Hang on, it should be the other way round. I'm the one who's pleased to meet you.' I have met a lot of the players who have meant something to me over the years and it has been a privilege.

BILL PATERSON: A few people didn't like George Best, who seemed to be right out on the edge of everything, but I have immense admiration for him. I have friends who are friends with him and they tell me he is a good man. I love Denis Law, another colourful type. I loved seeing him and I love hearing him because he has this lovely mixture of Aberdeen and Manchester in his voice and he is still a man of integrity. Bobby Charlton, too; that was the generation, the post-war generation, who made for an interesting approach because they knew how much football had given them; they hadn't reached the stage where they thought it was to be expected. Somebody told me the other day that George had never earned more than £1,000 a week, which sounds a lot for those days but it's pennies compared with what very average players pull in now.

WILLIE YOUNG: There have been times when I have felt like applauding some act of skill on the field. One game, Celtic v. Aberdeen, Paolo di Canio was wearing his golden boots and from a long clearance from defence he was in the centre-forward position. As the ball dropped on him from quite a height, he flicked it over the centre-half's head, ran round him and toe-poked it into the net. What a goal. You say to yourself, what a privilege to see that. Paolo was very volatile. In one game against Hearts he kneeled down in front of me and started to pray. I refereed his first Old Firm game at Ibrox and this is how much he

What a card: Referee Willie Young got on with Paul Gascoigne on and off the field. (Photo courtesy of Willie Young)

knew: the ball went into the crowd and it was a Celtic throw and Paolo ran off the field, over the track and into the Rangers crowd to collect the ball. I said: 'Are you mad? Do you want to get killed?'

Gascoigne and Laudrup were fantastic. Because of their career stage we tend not to get foreign players at their peak but Gascoigne and Laudrup were brilliant. Larsson is fantastic, too. Another Paolo, Maldini, was the guy who stands out for me; it looked as though he could play anywhere.

GEORGE ORMISTON: The players trained once a week and if they lived out of the area they would train with another team.

There was no pre-match warming-up and basically they just got changed and went out on to the field. They didn't even train with a ball half the time, just ran or maybe used a medicine ball. John White was the first player I remember doing a warm-up and he would do a limbering-up routine in the dressing-room before the game. John White was from Musselburgh and he played junior football for Bonnyrigg Rose. A scout who was a relation of John's mentioned him and he came out here for a trial. I remember

John White in his Alloa days.
(Photo courtesy of Willie McKie)

that trial match and it was obvious he was way ahead of the rest not just with football ability but with his brain. He was a very quiet lad. Scouts were here every week and because he wasn't a flashy type of player some didn't think much of him. Big Jimmy Smith, who was a scout for Rangers at the time, reckoned he would never make the grade.

WILLIE McKIE: I would be working in the dressing-rooms and John would never say two words; in fact he hardly said one most of the time. But an exceptional footballer, always two or three steps ahead of his teammates and the opposition. Two or three years back I got a phone call from someone representing John's sister and they were going to write a book about him.

GEORGE ORMISTON: If I remember, John's parents were deceased and an uncle had brought him up. His brother Eddie played here and the other brother Tommy played in his testimonial at White Hart Lane after John was killed by lightning. Other famous Alloa players: Dennis Gillespie who played with John White, went to Dundee United and got a League cap for Scotland. Tommy Hutchison started here, this was his first League club before he went on to play for Coventry and Scotland. He went from here to Blackpool where the manager was Stan Mortensen.

WILLIE McKIE: Tommy Hutchinson, of course, was famous for scoring a goal at both ends in the English Cup final. Even early on we could spot his talent, all arms and legs and very difficult to dispossess. I think he played on into his 40s.

LAWRIE REILLY: Gordon Smith was my hero and still is. He was so good that even when he didn't play well he still looked good. He was like a thoroughbred; when Gordon ran he looked like a sprinter, whereas the rest of us looked like Clydesdales, so even then he got a good press. Gordon was very much a loner, the other four forwards used to have a card school, playing for a penny or twopence, but Gordon used to sit in the corner and read a book; he wasn't a great mixer. In fact, to tell the honest truth, the only fault I would find with the Hibs was that he shouldn't have been captain of the team. A captain should be a bloke like Davie Shaw who used to play full-back and who would shout a lot and encourage you. Gordon never, ever did anything. He tossed the coin and that was the only reason you knew Gordon was the captain of the team. I also think captains again should be blokes that play in the middle of the park.

CRAIG BROWN: Gordon Smith was a wonderful gentleman. I was very nervous when I was in the team. We were on a tour of Iceland and Gordon was No. 7 in the team and I was No. 6, so it was obvious who I was going to be beside in the dressing-room. He put his hand on my knee and he said, 'Look, relax, son.' The previous evening we had had a discussion in the hotel about shaving and razor blades and Gordon had said to me: 'I've got the best razor that money can possibly buy. It's a Ronson, an electric razor,' probably quite expensive in those days, the early '60s. Now, I had expressed an interest in this razor and Gordon said to me before this match, 'Look, son, you have a good game today and I will give you a present.' So I played reasonably and then, when we got back home, the next game at Dens Park, I walked in the dressing-room and there in my place was a brand new Ronson with a note on it saying: 'Well done, Craig.' Well you can imagine the amount of encouragement that gave to a young lad.

There were other great characters in that team. Alex Hamilton was one. Alex used to pick the Scotland International Ugly Team. He would have Wigham of Falkirk in goals, right-back Shearer of Rangers, right-half Murdoch of Celtic and then he would come to centre-half and say Ian Ure, captain of the Ugly Team. Then he would pick the Scotland International Good-Looking Team: Bobby Brown of Rangers in goal and Alex Hamilton, Dundee and Scotland . . . captain. That team got to the semi-final of the European Cup, and beat Cologne, the champions of Europe, 8–1 at Dundee. It had Bobby Seith and Bert Slater was the goalkeeper. Many commentators, highly respected commentators, too, believe that was the best club side Scotland

Mister Memory: Bob Crampsey (pictured here with Pat Nevin) has seen Scottish football's glories. (© *Daily Record*/Mirrorpix)

ever produced, better than the Celtic side that won the European Cup. Bob Crampsey, who has seen everything, says that was the best club side he ever saw.

JOHN LAMBIE: Jock Stein, when he was with Clydebank, he would look at my team and say that's where all the headbangerss are. Lambie's team have all the headbangers. I got the name for that. The headbangers are the ones who have put me where I am in football. Chic Charnley is a superb guy. Harum-scarum, but he tells you the truth and I always tell players, don't ever tell me a lie, tell me the truth. I've had them all here, Dinnie, he's in jail but you should see the letters he gets here. John McNaught when he played for me at Hamilton before he transferred to Chelsea was from Easterhouse and a big harum-scarum guy. I used to phone him up on a Friday night. He stayed with his granny and she'd tell me he was round at his brother's. I phoned at midnight. No answer. I jumped in the car, drove round there and he wasn't there. Next day I faced him in the dressing-room and had it out with him and virtually told him: 'If you don't give me a shift today you'll never kick a ball again.' He was the star man. Outstanding he was. What a player. But he was a headbanger, he'd have fought with Goliath, he didn't give a care for anything in the world. Chic used to come in and try and get more bonuses for the players and then say: 'On a personal note, I think I should get a rise.'

I would just sit there and laugh at him. Ha, ha, ha. He didn't know what to do.

Pitman, him and Dinnie missed the plane when we were playing at Metz. Jim Oliver was chairman and said: 'What are we going to do?'

I said, 'Leave the so-and-sos.' And we did.

But these headbangers would give you blood and sweat. Chic would run for ever. I got him three times because they couldn't handle him. Never had a moment's trouble with him. You have to treat him as a man, not a kid.

Ray Montgomerie was a great professional, these are the guys who got us out of the Second Division. It's not about John Lambie, it's about the players. The funny thing is, I've six who left football and joined the polis!

I was going to pack it in a year ago because my health wasn't the best, but I knew people would cry me a coward so I gave it another year. This has been one of my biggest joys taking Partick through the leagues over four years and keeping them in the Premier League last season. Partick fans are unbelievable. Like fans everywhere they take to some players and not others, but the fans here do give players a chance. As far as I'm concerned, I can't speak highly enough of them.

SAMMY THE TAMMY: The Pars had some great characters. Norrie McCathie, obviously, Smudger Paul Smith, Shaggy Jenkins and John Watson. Paul Smith at the time was very undervalued, a strong midfielder and a good ball winner. When we lost him people would ask what was wrong and I would say, it's simple, we are missing the fight and the dig that Smudger gave us. Next best as a strong, hard-tackling midfielder was Ian Ferguson. Norrie was well known in the town and on the park he was inspirational. He would run upfield and beat three or four guys and then either trip over the ball, give it away or come up with a brilliant pass. One of three outcomes. The fans loved him. Any time the ball came near the 18-yard box it was his, he would just clear it. The night Norrie died I went along to the club and there were thousands of floral tributes. It was very emotional and very moving and even the non-football fans in the town felt his loss. At the service his mum made a speech and it was so moving. They laid out all the floral tributes on the pitch and they literally were bigger than the 18–yard box. Right now, Sammy is a huge fan of Craig Brewster, who has everything you want in a football player – skill to hold the ball, skill to lay the ball off, win everything in the air and a strong, aggressive player without being dirty. He also has remarkable touch for a big guy and scores some great goals. Sammy knows most of the players and has a great bit of banter with Scott Thomson, one of the most underrated players in Scotland; how he has never got a representative game is beyond me. It's outrageous.

JOHN LAMBIE: Eddie Turnbull was one of best three coaches in the world and the seven years at Hibs were the finest in my life. They did things in style and there was no stress or strain. We were going to all the European matches, and had Stanton, Brownlie and Blackley, even though they were all fading at that time. Des Bremner, no one had an engine like him, and I've had thousands of players under me. One minute defending in the box, next minute up the other end, fantastic, unbelievable. Chic would be high on my all-time list of favourites. He has always got a smile, nothing gets him down. And Albert Craig, a wee crabby so-and-so but a great player. I bought Albert for £10,000 and sold him for £100,000. Brian Martin, I got him for £30,000 and sold him for £110,000.

STUART COSGROVE: If I had to bring it down to one player it would be Sergei Baltacha, who was our sweeper. A big posse of us were out in Spain watching Scotland play what was then the USSR and they beat us 2–1. In that match was the famous incident when Hansen and Miller clashed and it was Baltacha who sent the ball through. You are thinking: 'Willie Miller, one of the greatest defenders Britain ever produced and Alan Hansen one of the classiest defenders in Britain,' but the real class on the park that day was Baltacha. When he arrived

Sergei Baltacha: Time on the ball and time in his Skoda. (© Louis Flood Photographers, Perth)

he came with nothing. He was in the Red Army and came with his tiny kids. Sergei Junior went on to play for his local school and St Mirren, and I think he is down at Millwall now and, of course, Elena became a tennis star. In a way they became a Saintee family.

He always seemed to have an extra ten minutes on the ball and you always had the feeling that he had been in every predicament before and knew how to get out of it. He'd be trapped in the corner and he would just feint, move the ball sideways and leave two players. There were times near the end when you thought he could have attacked the guys in the box and hammered them, but it wasn't his game. His game was about eloquence and I thought he was one of the greatest players I have had the privilege of seeing . . . and he was playing for St Johnstone. Some say he was

140

at the end of his career, but from my point of view he was at the beginning!

ALEX TOTTEN: When I signed Sergei Baltacha for St Johnstone we had agreed the terms and everything when he announced that he wanted a car as part of the deal and I thought: 'Oh no, he's going to want a Jag or a BMW or something like that.' But he wanted a Skoda. There's big Sergei, driving round Perth in his Skoda.

STUART COSGROVE: The fanzine has done a list of the top 100 Saints players of all time and I love telling Ally McCoist when I see him from time to time that he didn't make the top 20. Not even a sniff! Number one was Roddy Grant, then Baltacha, McLaren and a lot of great players. Super Ally? He wasn't even the top scorer when he played for Saints, John Brogan was.

WILLIE YOUNG: By and large Scottish players play by the book, and there is little outright cheating or feigning – that's a southern European thing. But I have had the pleasure of sending off Ally McCoist, although he was only playing for Kilnockie, in a Robert Duval film.

ALEX McLEISH: At the top level now, players have achieved superstar status. Whether money has changed them along the way I don't know. They have a cult status and I would probably need a letter of introduction to get close to David Beckham these days, never mind you! Like every entertainer, there has to be a mystique about them, but let's face it, they still all play with a round ball and a pair of shorts whether they are superstars or kids in the park.

3

90 MINUTES

LAWRIE REILLY: I was standing at the bus stop going down to play for Hibs against Manchester United at a game at Easter Road and a fellow came up to me and says: 'Congratulations, I see you've been picked to play for the Scottish League.' It was in the stop press that I was in the team to play the League of Ireland. I didn't know whether to run back and tell my mum and dad, who wouldn't have seen the paper. So that's how I found out, from a fellow with a newspaper saying: 'See you're picked to play for the Scottish League.'

My mum and dad saw me in every game from juvenile right to Scotland internationals. I scored the first time I went to Wembley. It's always great to score when you're playing in big games like that but I got more enjoyment out of making the first goal for Jimmy Mason because he had done so much for me. The first goal Jimmy scored, I went down the left and cut it across and wee Mason hit it. I got more enjoyment out of that than any other goal I've scored. He played with Third Lanark, who weren't a big club. If he had played for the like of Rangers he would have been one of the greats of Scottish football.

We could beat most teams but we had a hell of hard job beating the Hearts. There was one game against the Hearts and I happened to score a hat-trick. We beat them 3–1 and Bobby Parker, the Hearts right-back, scored with a penalty kick. The headline in the *Evening News* said: 'Parker Penalty Fails to Save Hearts.' You would have thought it would be 'Reilly Hat-trick Wins the Game', but no.

GORDON BROWN: I remember 1963 when we were beaten 9–3 by England and Frank Haffey was the goalkeeper. He emigrated to Australia and the famous story was that he had met Denis Law over there several years later and asked him if it was safe to come home yet. Denis told him no!

CRAIG LEVEIN: I got my first Scotland cap in 1990. I wasn't long back from my injury, I had worked really hard to get back and in January 1990 we played Argentina at Hampden and we won 1–0. Stewart McKimmie got the goal and I was up against a young Claudio Caniggia, who has lasted a bit longer in the game than me! That was a wonderful experience, especially after almost three years on and off with problems with my knee, and never thinking I would get back in the position when I'd have the chance. I was also in a Scotland squad in 1986 under Alex Ferguson before they went to the World Cup; I was over in Israel before the final selection of the squad of 28, so that was a first taster for me and of course just after that I got injured. At my lowest point I never thought that I would get back and play for my country, but then I managed to get myself back into that position four years later. The Scotland thing was great. I went to the World Cup in 1990, and these were some of the proudest days of my life. We played Sweden in Genoa and coming out the tunnel I saw my brothers Paul and Gary in a mass of Scotland supporters. They were shouting, so I went across to have a word with them. What a wonderful experience.

That game, in which we beat Sweden 2–1, was the best and the biggest occasion I had been involved in. In the first game Costa Rica had beaten us 1–0, so Sweden was a really important game.

It really was something that was extra special. I would say that was the game I enjoyed. But then I had more problems with my knees and my ankles, and every time I seemed to get a run and have a few games in a row something else would happen. But mysterious things happen and if I hadn't got injured then I wouldn't have gone into coaching so quickly and I wouldn't be sat here as manager of Hearts, the club I spent most of my career with – and we are talking 14 years.

DAVID McGREGOR: I can remember that match that clinched promotion in '84 against Stranraer as if it was yesterday. I've got a video of it in the house, actually. Stranraer took the lead in the second minute and Sam Smith, the chairman, turned to us all and said: 'Well, gentlemen, that certainly wasn't in the script.' We won 5–3 that day. That was also our centenary year.

IAN WILSON: I had five caps for Scotland. I played in a B international against France at Aberdeen and was a bit fortunate because of a few cry-offs. It was the first time I had been back at Pittodrie and I was playing against a certain Eric Cantona who was making his debut for France at the time and stood out a mile. Then I got in the senior squad and played against England and Brazil, and Bulgaria in a World Cup qualifier.

My father was alive and he saw me play against England and Brazil in 1987 and within 12 months he died. But at least he had had the pride of seeing me in a Scotland jersey.

Brothers at arms: Ian Wilson and Charlie Nicholas played in the same Scotland side. (Photo courtesy of Peterhead FC)

DAVE MACKAY: I won 22 caps and would have had a lot more had I not been injured but even at that we didn't get too many favours in terms of caps. Willie Bauld, Lawrie Reilly, Gordon Smith and guys like that got very few caps.

IAIN PAXTON: Raith Rovers had that brilliant time when Jimmy Nicholl was there in the '90s and what they achieved was unbelievable really. The first season I had stopped playing rugby at Selkirk and I used to go to Stark's Park, because rather than watch rugby I wanted to do something different. I would just have tied myself up in knots watching rugby. They won the new First Division to get into the Premier League, Peter Hetherston was the captain and they had a whole host of good players like Colin Cameron, Stevie Crawford and Dave Sinclair, who went down to Millwall. They got to the Coca-Cola Cup final where they beat Celtic, which was undoubtedly the highlight of my days as a Raith Rovers supporter. I have still got the programme upstairs in a bookcase beside the bed.

The only other cup I saw them win was the Fife Cup when they beat East Fife, which was not quite the same thing. But that was packed full of incident and the cup must have been taken up and down the tunnel about three times. It was 2–1 to East Fife going into injury time and the trophy was out for East Fife. Then it was 2–2 and then Rovers scored another goal and the trophy was back out. It was quite comical seeing this trophy going up and down the tunnel with different ribbons on it.

The Coca-Cola Cup year, I hadn't seen any games because I was coaching rugby, which tended to take up a lot of my week. I remember coming back from rugby training at Glenrothes in the car – I think they had beaten Airdrie in the semi-final and I am sure it was at McDiarmid Park. It went to injury time and then penalties just as we were crossing the Forth Bridge, and we just about put the car over the bridge when Rovers got the deciding penalty.

But in those days we did use to give the Old Firm a doing – we were their bogey team. It goes back to 1971 when we last beat the Old Firm home and away in the same season with guys like John Connolly, who later went to Everton. I was 17 at the time and just going to university and you are thinking: oh, Rangers this weekend, that's three points in the bag. You knew you could beat them. Aberdeen were a bigger worry in those days.

DAVID McGREGOR: Arbroath and Brechin are traditional derby matches. It's a strange thing, although Montrose is in Angus as well it's never been quite looked upon with the same fervour. Montrose has just never had the same ring to it and I cannot think of the reason for that.

IAN BLACK: Stranraer v. Queen of the South is our local derby. It's 80 miles away, but there will always be a big rivalry between the two teams and for a good number of years recently Stranraer had the upper hand, believe it or not. They were able to beat us, no problem, and it's just basically the last couple of years that we've turned it back round again. You don't get the same coverage down in Dumfries as, say, your Rangers, St Mirren, Falkirk or other teams in the central belt. A lot of people seem to forget about us unless we're doing something, but up until the last couple of seasons we basically didn't get any coverage in the newspapers – there were maybe four or five lines for the match report. Like every other town in Scotland local football fans seem to want to go and watch Celtic and Rangers and not support their local team. A lot of people who were Queen of the South fans had enough watching Queens. But I know people who have come back again; they can't afford to go and watch Celtic and Rangers any more.

FRANK McAVEETY: The first big game for me was the St Johnstone v. Celtic Cup final in 1969, when I was six. Bertie Auld scored in the third minute while my father was still in the pub and I didn't even see the goal. My father used to find his way into the ground about five, six minutes into the game, so I have a faint memory of a boring game, Celtic having won it in the first few minutes. The more interesting games were the first big European matches, like Celtic against Basle, and probably the most exciting game for me as a teenager was the night before my economics higher, when I should have been studying and allowed myself to be seduced into going to Celtic Park for a big decider against Rangers. Celtic had to win and they did – 4–2. I arrived at my economics higher the next day without any voice, that was my memory of that one. In those days there was a big slope at the Celtic end – you're walking up the steps and looking down the slope, and just realising that it's a big stadium for a wee boy. Dad was always late at getting there. I stood at the top end and I was up on his shoulders for most of the game to try and see.

LORD MACFARLANE: I give a gallon bottle of BELL'S® at the end of the season to the chairman of the club with the best pies. East Fife have won it for the last two years, Clyde won it the previous year and St Mirren the year before that. The press are very interested. They phone me up during the year when there's no news and say, 'Who is winning the pie competition?' I am the sole judge and I eat a pie every Saturday. It's about the crispness of the outer crust very often, it has to be heated to the proper temperature and nicely presented. That's how I judge it. It gives the club something to talk about. At half-time when I'm having my pie and my cup of tea in the club I'm always approached by people who say: 'How is it?'

GORDON BROWN: I was 16 in 1967 when Scotland humbled England on their own turf, thanks in large part to Jim Baxter. It was a home international and a European Championship qualifier but of course to many Scots it is still regarded as the real

World Cup decider. Many Scots' pride in their team's performances has been enhanced periodically by defeating the English at the game they regard as their own and there is still a pub in central Scotland that proudly displays a lump of turf taken from Wembley after the 2–1 win in 1977. I have travelled far with Scotland. I was in Seville for Narey's toe-poke in 1982 and in Italy in 1990. In Genoa, as the Italians prepared for the invasion of the Tartan Army, Scotland beat Sweden 2–1 and there was never any trouble.

Wem-ber-lee, Wem-ber-lee: Scotland celebrate after the 1967 victory over world champions England at Wembley. Left to right: Bobby Lennox, Billy Bremner, Tommy Gemmell, Jim McCalliog, Eddie McCreadie and Jim Baxter. (© *Daily Record*/Mirrorpix)

DOUGRAY SCOTT: Anfield when Scotland put Wales out of the World Cup is the match that stands out for me. I wasn't there, but I watched it on the telly. The other one that sticks in my mind is another qualifier when Scotland scored the most horrendous own-goal at Hampden I can remember. I've been to quite a lot of Scotland matches, but I can't recall a dafter own-goal.

ALLAN GRIEVE: The whole season of 1995–96 was incredible. At one point we went 27 games without defeat. We were going to places like Queen of the South and winning 7–0 and we went to Forfar and won 6–0. We had an absolutely outstanding side that season, the best Stirling Albion team that I've ever seen.

As for special matches, over the years we've been involved in a lot of really exciting, unusual one-off games. The Scottish Cup

Scott Maxwell makes it 2–0 to Stirling Albion against Selkirk.
Final score 20–0. (Photo courtesy of Allan Grieve)

tie against Selkirk in 1984. An amazing League Cup tie with
Celtic in 1980. The Selkirk match was the biggest scoreline in
any professional football match in Britain in the twentieth
century. The record wins in the record books are things like 36–0
for Arbroath but they were all in the nineteenth century. No
other team won by more than 16–0 in the twentieth century. So
our 20–0 was an absolutely phenomenal achievement. It was only
5–0 at half-time as well. Fifteen goals shooting down the slope at
Annfield in the second half. Just by coincidence the BBC actually
filmed that game – they were making a documentary about the
Scottish Cup – so we got a video of the whole match. So we
actually looked at the video afterwards and at one point we scored
eight goals in a twelve–minute spell in the second half. A couple
of players did not manage to get on the scoresheet. The
goalkeeper was one, and Jimmy Sinclair, who is now director of
youth football with the SFA, was the other. A great guy, Jimmy;
he won't thank me for saying he never ever scored for Stirling
Albion in any of the games and he still didn't manage to score in

that game. He played midfield but needless to say it was midfield and tracking back all the time. David Thompson scored seven in that game and Willie Irvine scored five.

IAN BLACK: The day we won the Second Division Championship in 2001–02 when we came home that night, we had always said when Queens win a trophy we would climb Robert Burns' statue in Dumfries town centre and put a Queens scarf round his neck, and that's what we did that night. The police caught us but they just laughed and let us go. We had had two or three pints of shandy. Burns spent more of his life in Dumfries than Ayrshire and I like to think he would have been a Queens fan. If he had been alive that night, he would certainly have been drinking with us.

A game's a game for a' that: Robbie Burns was a Queen of the South fan for one night. (Photo courtesy of Dumfries & Galloway Tourist Board)

ALLAN GRIEVE: As for the the Celtic game, a League Cup tie was played over two legs in those days. The first leg was at Annfield, on a Wednesday night, and against all the odds we beat Celtic 1–0. Lloyd Irvine scored and we played well but over two legs you thought, OK, we've won 1–0, but we go to Parkhead four days later really expecting to be well beaten. We went to Parkhead and, lo and behold, after 15 minutes, we scored, so we were now 2–0 up on aggregate. Celtic pulled one goal back before half-time and the second-half went on and on and on. We were winning 2–1 on aggregate and it was absolutely desperate last-ditch defending. We never had an attack, we were never out of our own half, but we held out until two minutes to go when Celtic scored, making it 2–1 and taking it to extra-time. Of course by that time we were just out on our feet and we finished up losing 6–1 in extra-time, but it was so close. It would have been an incredible result over two legs.

Celtic had Pat Bonner, who was in goals, Danny McGrain, people like that, and in extra-time they brought on a youngster who had hardly played at that time and he came on and scored a couple of goals in extra-time in his first game for Celtic. His name was Charlie Nicholas.

Later that season, we saw the opposite end of the spectrum. At the start of the season we had beaten Celtic, we beat Falkirk in the League, we had great results and the last game on 31 January 1981, we went to Dunfermline and we won 1–0, with a last-minute goal from Matt McPhee. Things were looking good, but unfortunately we didn't score another goal until August. That's right, we went the whole of February, March, April and a couple of games in May, and never scored. We did manage to score in the first game of the new season in August. Fair enough, we lost 4–1, but scoring a goal was enough. We didn't actually win another game until the end of September and we went from the end of January until the end of September without winning, January to August without scoring. We hold a few records of the type. It's actually incredible, I mean towards the end of that run we played Hamilton Accies at Annfield and a guy played up front for us at that time, Graham Armstrong, who twice rounded the goalkeeper, had an open goal and missed! Unbelievable, he couldn't have done it, missed, if he tried. The second-last game of the season, away to St Johnstone, we got a penalty, and missed that, too! It seemed we were fated never to score again. St Johnstone, they actually got promoted that day; they beat us 1–0 and a young Ally McCoist scored that goal.

BRIAN FLYNN: The best team Falkirk had was probably '72 when Alex Ferguson played for us. In 1971–72 we got to the Scottish Cup, the League Cup semi-final against Partick Thistle and we won the League. I must have been 14 or 15 when we played Rangers in the Scottish Cup. They were beating us 2–1 when Fergie went through and scored the equaliser with about five minutes to go. I was a big lad, but my dad swears to this day he lifted me shoulder high and put me on his shoulders and we were all jumping about.

Another one was against Aberdeen, with Fergie, as he does as a manager, diving in the box for a penalty and getting it, and I always remember he had these elbows, the elbows were his tools of the trade. He was terrific, he did really well and scored a lot of goals for us.

FRANK McAVEETY: I saw the 1970 Gordon Banks save on a black and white telly, but it's the brilliance of that Brazilian side that sticks even though I was only eight years of age. That must be the best side anyone alive can genuinely say they have ever seen. There were eight or nine of those players who were all class. One of them, the defender Piazza, I used to to quote during the speeches. He was asked, 'How did you feel about playing in this great side with the likes of Pelé and Jairzinho?' and he said something like, 'It's a little bit like the little humming bird that takes water in its beak when the forest is on fire, it takes water from the river and drops it on the fire and the wise old bird says: "Why are you doing that?" and the humming bird says: "I'm only doing my part."' I think it's an old folk tale from his history and he used it to define his role. Because no one remembers him.

TERRY CHRISTIE: The duffle coat. I actually used to have a Crombie coat but it got soaked standing on the terracing. I was raking about in the cupboard and my son Max had bought a duffle coat that he had never worn, and I said, 'Max, you never wear this duffle coat I'm going to take it,' so I started with the duffle coat and nobody paid any attention, but we beat Aberdeen and it was on television and the duffle coat became a sign and now I'm quite attached to it. It's actually duffle mark 2. I'm waiting for a new one to come this season.

BRIAN FLYNN: The 1997 Cup run was unbelievable. We famously beat Celtic in the replay at Ibrox after Kevin James scored the equaliser on the Saturday and we went through again on the Wednesday night, thinking, 'Ah well, you only get one chance', but we scored an early goal and we held on and on. In the final, we thought that against Kilmarnock history was on our side. We had beaten them 40 years earlier, after all. But we lost a goal and then had a goal, which was never offside in a million years, chopped off but the linesman put his flag up. We lost the Cup when at that point we had been in the game; I think Kilmarnock would probably have caved if we had equalised. I've got the whole game on tape and I've never watched it, I could never bring myself to watch it. I've seen bits and pieces of highlights, but there were 20,000 Falkirk fans at Ibrox that day and you wonder where they all go on a Saturday; it was wonderful. We weren't really disappointed after the game until we saw the European draw for Kilmarnock.

RICHARD GORDON: My mum refused to allow me to travel to Glasgow for the Cup final in 1970. She is from the west coast and I think she just had this fear of her wee boy loose in the big city, so my dad went to the game instead. But I do remember listening in. My mum took me shopping, but we were on the bus and it had a radio on so I could hear it, then we were in a shop and it came over the tannoy system that Aberdeen had beaten Celtic 3–1. The Dons were massive underdogs as it was still virtually the Lisbon Lions who were playing for Celtic and it was such a thrill, my first really big

1970 Scottish Cup final between Aberdeen and Celtic.
(Photo courtesy of Aberdeen FC)

thrill in football. My dad arrived home late at night with the match programme and as I was leafing though it, it was a phenomenal experience. There were lots of stories about that team, Martin Buchan was 21 and the youngest-ever captain to lift the Scottish Cup. His brother George was a substitute – unused, but you've got the family connection there. That's the team that always stuck with me from then on. In my first season as a supporter they won a trophy and for the next 15 years won nothing. But that ignited it. The next season, 1970–71, I certainly didn't miss a home game and my dad took me to quite a few away games and they very nearly won the league. That was my first heartbreak as a football fan. They pushed Celtic all the way. My dad actually took me down to Celtic Park, where Aberdeen won 1–0, in the December of 1970. That was my first time in Glasgow and I still remember standing there and being surrounded by this huge mass of people, because there was no segregation of rival fans.

ARTHUR MONTFORD: I worked in journalism when I came out of the Army in 1949 and got a job on the local paper at Coatbridge, where I met Jock Stein, who was a player for Albion Rovers at the time. My long-standing friendship with Jock began there and over the years he and I got on very well. I remember doing an interview with him before the 1961 Cup final when his Dunfermline side were due to face Celtic, and I said to him: 'You are working hard with these players,' and he replied, 'Yes, they are average Scottish players but they've got talent and it's my job to make sure they use that talent.' That was his basic philosophy throughout his managerial career. I interviewed the Dunfermline players, who he gave me great access to, and I sensed they might just cause an upset. It took, of course, a world-class performance from Eddie Connachan to keep Celtic at bay but then they famously won the replay 2–0. I followed the team back to Dunfermline with the band playing, on the top.

RICHARD GORDON: At the end of the season we were playing Celtic at home in the second-last game of the season and a victory would all but clinch the league. Celtic had a corner within the first three minutes and Harry Hood headed it in; 1–0 Celtic. I sat there and just burst into tears. I got no sympathy from my dad, I have to say. I think he was just embarrassed that his son was crying. Aberdeen equalised, then, in the second half, Arthur Graham, one of my great heroes, broke free of the Celtic defence bearing in on goal, went round Williams, the Celtic goalkeeper, and just as he was going round him Williams got a touch of the ball and knocked it away. Graham doubled back and then just spun round and knocked it towards goal. It had to go in, but he didn't get enough pace on it and Billy McNeill came back and cleared it off the line. It was 1–1. That's how close we came. It all ended in tears again when the following week Dad took me down to Brockville and we lost to Falkirk in the final game of the season, and Celtic won the League by two points. With having won the cup in the first season, the next year going well to win the League, it was devastating at the time, just awful. I still remember that day so clearly – getting off the train and walking down to Brockville Stadium. Davie Robb handled the ball and gave away a penalty, and George Miller, who was the Falkirk stalwart, scored the penalty.

DOUGRAY SCOTT: I've got a season ticket and I went to about eight games last season and maybe 11 games the season before. I go when I get a chance, when I'm not filming. I went to see Hibs in Athens against AEK Athens and then to the second leg at Easter Road, and that was the best the Hibs have played at Easter Road for years. They were phenomenal that night, absolutely wonderful. Sauzee just played out of his skin – he was always great for us Franck Sauzee, but that night, particularly, he was

Alex McLeish with Dougray Scott at Athens airport in 2001, where Hibs travelled to play AEK Athens in the first round, first leg of the UEFA Cup.
(© The Scotsman Publications Limited)

outstanding. When I went down to Wales to college, the only matches I went to were still Hibs matches when I was at home for holidays and even now I love football and I love watching it. I would much rather watch the Scottish Premier League game than the English one, even if the football is much better in England. Some of the football in England is fantastic, but I can't get as passionate about it because I don't have an English team that I support; I'm a Hibs fan and I've only got room really for one team. But I like going to live matches. I've been to Chelsea a few times and I've been to Fulham a few times, but if I've got the time to go and see a football match I'd much rather get on the plane and go up to Scotland.

RICHARD GORDON: The first final I broadcast live was the 1991 League Cup final when Hibs beat Dunfermline 2–0 at Hampden, and that was before Hampden was redeveloped. We were in the old press box in the corner in a wee cubbyhole opening up the windows and hanging out and trying to soak up the atmosphere. Murdo MacLeod, who I work with now, was captain of Hibs. Then I covered the great League Cup final of 1994, when Raith Rovers beat Celtic on penalties at Ibrox and we followed Rovers on their UEFA Cup run the following season when Chic Young and I stuck with them throughout.

Bayern Munich came to Easter Road and Rovers lost that one 2–0 but the big thrill was being in the stadium in Munich with them. We got to know the players. Wee Jimmy Nicoll's a great guy and we also got to meet a lot of the fans, and we just wanted them to have success. I'll never forget Danny Lennon's freekick being deflected into the roof of the net and Chic and I sitting there at half-time looking up at this huge screen which read 'Bayern Munich 0 Raith Rovers 1' and there were guys all round taking photographs of it – just fantastic.

Another that sticks in the mind is the opening game of the World Cup in France in 1998, when Scotland faced Brazil. Just

Colin Hendry challenges Ronaldo for the ball during the World Cup game between Scotland and Brazil in 1998. (© *Daily Record*/Mirrorpix)

being there. I had been at the World Cup in 1994, but Scotland hadn't been involved, and 1998 was our first real big coverage of the World Cup finals with Scotland there and they were kicking the tournament off against the favourites! Ronaldo had just come to the fore, so there was this huge anticipation about him. I remember seeing the guys walking on to the pitch beforehand and it was just such a colourful spectacle, a wonderful occasion. We went behind, then John Collins got the penalty and it was another of those scoreboard moments. Then, in typical Scottish fashion, we lose it the only way imaginable – Tom Boyd chesting the ball into his own net. But that match was a fantastic thrill. More recently, being out in Seville with Celtic that whole three days, hooped jerseys absolutely everywhere, was another memorable experience. They figured about 76,000 Celtic fans made the trip, which apparently beat the previous record of Manchester United in 1999, with 51,000 at the Nou Camp. The Celtic fans partied non-stop for three days.

PETER DONALD: My wife will say that I can see 25 seconds of action on TV and say that was such and such and wee Willie will score at the end of this. She thinks that's unbelievable, but I just think anybody who is interested in football has that kind of recall. I went to see Scotland for the first time in the mid-'60s, to various games that were played here, and all the huge attendances on the terraces at Hampden. I can remember going to see all the Scotland games and travelling on the football special from Central Station to Mount Florida. Everybody travelled on the football specials in those days, as they didn't have the cars; others just walked out.

I went to the traditional Wembley game the year after England won the World Cup in 1967 and we got a special bus from Johnstone, well from a small village called Kilbarchan actually, and the first stop was the toilets in Johnstone Square – a journey of about four minutes.

RICHARD GORDON: I desperately wanted Celtic to win in Seville and it was such a disappointment at the end. As we were going into extra-time we looked at the Porto players and they all looked absolutely shocked and there was a real feeling of belief in the stadium that Celtic could do it. Then Balde got sent off and it all fell apart, but it was a great occasion. The Celtic fans sung throughout the game, and it wasn't until we got the bus back into the city centre and walked back to the hotel that it all sunk in. It was like everything had just fallen in on them, but it was great; I sat up all night, just chatting to the Celtic fans. They all had stories to tell and they will never forget it. It was such a disappointment that they didn't win but it was a trip and an occasion that will never be forgotten.

From a purely professional point of view the time I've broadcast is the only era in which Aberdeen haven't been winning anything. It just seems to me that the start of my broadcasting career coincided with them falling apart and it wasn't until 1995 that they beat Dundee 2–0 to win the League Cup final. That's a long wait. To be there on the day, on air when we had won the

League Cup, that was a great moment. To be honest everybody knows whom I support, but when I'm on air I try to be as unbiased as possible. If anything, I think I am probably over-critical of Aberdeen, certainly I was during the Ebbe Skovdahl period. I got a lot of stuff from fans saying I was blinkered about Skovdahl, which I could never quite understand.

ARTHUR MONTFORD: Earlier, in 1959, we followed St Mirren on 'The Road To Hampden', where they beat Aberdeen 3–1 in the final, and we went back to Paisley with them and, of course, having had access to the team and the manager all through it was just a fairy-tale ending for us. Those were the good days on television.

PETER DONALD: People are quite proud of going on the Wembley pitch and digging up the turf. I'm actually quite embarrassed by all that, which is maybe why I became a football administrator. I just want to leave the park to the players and I want to see what they are doing at the end of the game, I just don't want any interference. It's their day; your place is on the terrace.

ARTHUR MONTFORD: I did something like 2,000 *Scotsport*s or thereabouts. Some 400 commentaries, 28 or 29 Rangers–Celtic games, World Cup qualifiers, World Cup openers, World Cup finals, so I was lucky enough, and *Scotsport* were lucky enough to be busy and active. Scotland were qualifying for all those World Cups in the '70s and '80s, and that gave us many great programmes, and there was nothing quite as exciting as those live nights when your country qualifies for the World Cup: Scotland v. Czechoslovakia and Scotland v. Wales are just two that spring to mind – totally memorable games – and there was a great passion about the crowd and the team. Somebody asked me recently: 'Why is it we don't have the spirit of the '70s any more?' Only partially tongue in cheek, I said it's to do with the jerseys – the jerseys are not dark blue enough with the lion and nothing else on them. They've got stripes, they don't look like Scottish jerseys. A dark blue jersey with a collar and a yellow lion is a Scottish jersey. That's maybe not the reason why, but I still think that the proper jersey helps the passion, brings the passion to it.

STUART COSGROVE: The 7–2 win was one of our best ever results against Dundee and one of the highlights of your life as a fan. Plus the fact that it was New Year, traditionally a time when fans return home from all over and make it back for the big derby. A derby at New Year on our ground was heaven sent to give them a licking. It was an incredible open game, with a lot of good football as the result suggests, but St Johnstone were way ahead of Dundee. The rivalry between the two clubs is ingrained in history.

Most people say it began in the early '60s when Dundee had to draw the last game of the 1961 season to win the Championship, but a draw would have suited St Johnstone because that meant we would have stayed in the old First Division; a defeat for us would relegate us and win them the Championship. I remember there were some very bad tackles, from a St Johnstone full-back on a Dundee striker, in particular, and according to Dundee players that soured the game. They decided they were going out to win the game and not play out a draw. So we got relegated in what was a bitter end-of-season game and they won the Championship. From then the fixture has had a history.

My uncle heard me explain this on the radio and he said it goes way beyond then. This is where it gets really bizarre: Perthshire, which in the old shire sense is actually bigger than Angus, which is Dundee's county, always had a better cricket team than Angus, so in midsummer St Johnstone football fans would go and support Perthshire because they were playing Dundee, and my uncle said that goes back to the '40s and '50s where you got an away day at Dundee on the back of being able to ride them at cricket as well.

Another person said to me there was another period, from the '80s onwards, of intense resentment. Perth is obviously a smaller town than Dundee, but in the past it was less socially deprived, so that when the local government changes came in the '80s and the country was divided into the Tayside region, the Grampian region, the Strathclyde region and so on, the regional headquarters became Dundee and not Perth and lot of public service workers in Perth had to commute to Dundee every day. You had a lot of Perth people really reluctantly having to travel to Dundee and there was the perception that Dundee was the boss and for five or six years this caused quite significant resentment.

Then, of course, Dundee United took off in Europe so Dundee had gone 20 or 30 years being the second team in Dundee. When they got relegated and St Johnstone got in the Premier League they had to cope with being the third-best team in Tayside. Beating them 7–2 that day was a phenomenal day and one that will live with me until the day I die.

WILLIE YOUNG: I was Eastern Europe correspondent for the SFA at one time – Ukraine, Lithuania, Belarus. In Lithuania, the electricity would go off about 9 p.m., whenever Russia got upset with them.

IAN WILSON: When I went to Elgin City, it was the best move I ever made. I got stronger, filled out a little bit and and we played Rangers in the quarter-final of the Scottish Cup. We got beat 3–0, but seeing all the famous players who were playing for Rangers at the time was an experience; Alex Macdonald, Sandy Jardine, Colin Stein, John Greig – big names at that time. I enjoyed that, it was a dream come true. The Elgin players couldn't believe how big the bath was; it even had steps up to it. At Elgin the bath was about six foot square but this was 15 yards square, a swimming pool.

PATRICK BARCLAY: When we won the League I thought it was always going to be like this. Unfortunately I never saw the 5–1 win at Ibrox. We were on a bus to go to Glasgow but turned back for some reason – faulty brakes or something like that. The following season, 1962–63, we played in the European Cup and that was really pinch-yourself stuff. We were drawn against Cologne and we thought that by some piece of luck we might just get through. We knew we were a good team, but never realised how good. Cologne were third favourites and we thought if we could manage a 1–1 draw at Dens and then maybe get beaten in Cologne that would be respectable. They had Karl-Heinz Schnellinger in the team, and so on. After 20 minutes we were 5–0 up. We won 8–1 and Alan Gilzean scored four goals. OK, a contributing factor was an injury to their goalkeeper, who was kicked in the head early on and of course there were no replacements in those days. In the second leg they kicked OUR goalkeeper and were 4–0 up at half-time in Cologne! Talk about comebacks. All they had to do was score another four goals in the second half and they were through and we were out. I saw the Sporting Lisbon game and I saw the Anderlecht game, but I think I missed the Milan game, the semi-final, because I couldn't get a ticket. But I went to the top of the Law and sat watching the floodlit ground and tried to feel a part of it. My best experience was the third round when we were drawn against possibly the greatest Anderlecht team of all time, with Paul Van Himst and some of the greatest Belgian players ever. We thought this was where it might all end.

In those days there was no chance of getting to Belgium for the away leg so I thought I would try and listen in on a radio station, and doing Dundee's game was probably not a high priority for the BBC so I was twiddling the knobs on this transistor radio and I must have come across a Flemish station because I couldn't understand a word. But it seemed like a football commentary. My heart just burst with joy because did this guy sound glum. He was saying things I could make out like 'Gilzean, ah nah', and I knew things were going well and I could hear the crowd were disconsolate and sure enough we won 4–1 and won the second leg 2–1. Unfortunately, it all came to an end in Milan but I was pinching myself by now. The final was at Wembley that year and if we had got there and won we would have been the first; forget Celtic, forget Manchester United, forget Matt Busby, forget Jock Stein, Alex Ferguson. Dundee FC would have become a British institution.

I thought it would always be like this. But then Gilly was sold to Spurs, Ian Ure was sold to Arsenal, Bob Shankly eventually left and the whole thing broke up.

FORDYCE MAXWELL: One of the questions I am always asked is if I saw the 1967 game when Berwick beat Rangers in the Scottish Cup and I didn't because I was down south watching Nottingham Forest beat Newcastle in the English Cup! I remember the impact that win had on the town, though. It got to be a bit like that European Cup final between Real Madrid and Eintracht Frankfurt; there were 135,000 at that match, but if you counted up everyone who said they had been there it would be more like a million. If you counted up all the people in Berwick who said they were at the 1967 game you'd probably have 50,000. But everybody in the town felt great and it lasted for a long time.

But I can say I was there for the 1960 game against Rangers and the abiding memory of that game was Rangers' Alex Scott racing down the wing and beating Charlie Beacham and, as he went past, Charlie grabbing his shorts before Scott went on down the wing in his jockstrap. There was a crowd of 13,000 for that game as it was before the limits so Scott got a big cheer from us for running down the wing in his jockstrap. The Rangers fans were really good-humoured, probably because they won, and I'm told they weren't like that for the 1967 game. But there was never any bother in those days. There wasn't a lot of money around and we would always stand behind the goal because it was cheaper.

Work stopped me from going for a long time but in the autumn of 1987 I started going back to Shielfield. We had changed the farming system, so there wasn't so much livestock and I had more spare time on a Saturday afternoon. I had this sudden, overwhelming urge that I had to see live football again. So I just drove into Berwick and have been most Saturdays since. You don't expect too much. They drew 0–0 with Rangers in a reprise of the 1967 game, a match in which the Berwick defence put up a terrific show, and then went to the replay at Ibrox, or Castle Greyskull as we call it. Rangers made it 1–0 and the Berwick fans began to sing 'We're going to win 2–1' and so on. When Rangers got to 3–0 they gave up on singing 'We're going to win 4–3', but it was good fun and there was something like 1,500 people went from Berwick that night. But crowds have gone down over the years. As for the 400 or so they get for some matches now we used to have bigger crowds than that in the local cup competitions, like the Charities Cup.

HUGH WALLACE: Last year, 2002, when the Champions League final was taking place at Hampden, I was approached by UEFA through the SFA to enquire as to whether they might use the church halls as an accreditation centre. It seemed a bit bizarre to see the Rocksteady Security people checking people coming in and out of the church! As part payment for this, UEFA provided us with two VIP tickets, which raised considerable funds for the church. For the first time since I have been minister at Mount Florida, the residents came out to soak in the pre-match atmosphere. Usually they leave the area until a match is over or stay indoors. The Real Madrid and Bayer Leverkusen supporters and the Glasgow people made 21 May 2002 a day to remember for those in the street as much as Zidane made his winner a match to remember for the crowd. Following on from that, I was invited by the SFA to act as an independent arbiter to ballot the Scotland travelling support who wished tickets for the match in Iceland. So there I was with the 'big man' (he's actually smaller than me!), Berti Vogts, in the SFA offices, ensuring that the allocation of tickets was done fairly. I have a photograph of myself with Berti which I will probably display more prominently once Scotland recover their winning ways!

WILLIE YOUNG: A cup tie at Kilwinning was probably the worst I ever handled. It was mayhem. I put three off and I lost count of the cautions I had given. Oddly enough there was an assessor at that game and he came into the room where I was sat with my head in my hands and congratulated me on my handling of the game. If he hadn't done that I would probably have quit there and then.

After the Edinburgh derby last year, when Hibs got a penalty in the last minute and won the game, some bright spark sent me a death threat . . . from his home email. So he is currently serving six months!

I have done a stack of Edinburgh derbies, Dundee derbies and Old Firm derbies and the commitment and the passion you get in those are bigger than anything you will get in a foreign game. Foreign games are easier to referee because the build-up is slower and more measured. We used to wear heart monitors and your heart rate was always higher in Scottish Premier League matches than it was in international matches.

WILLIE McKIE: It's easy to pick out an outstanding match: the 7–5 win against Queen's Park, a league match. We were 5–2 down at half-time.

GEORGE ORMISTON: I can still remember the manager Archie McPherson, the ex-Rangers and Sheffield United player, and the chairman Bob Beatson shouting at the team at half-time. It wasn't normal for the chairman to go in the dressing-room at half-time, but these seemed special circumstances.

WILLIE McKIE: We still speak to Peter Buchanan, who played for Queen's Park in that match. The ground had a slight slope and the great Alloa teams of the past liked to play downhill in the second half, and in that match they were playing downhill after the break towards the railway end. It doesn't come into play so much now because of the different fitness levels, but there is no doubt it was a big psychological weapon in those days.

SAMMY THE TAMMY: Ask any Pars fan and it will be the same one; the day we beat Dundee United on their own patch (1996–97), to secure promotion thanks to a toe-poke by Stewart Petrie in the seventh minute. The Pars fans were there for 25 minutes in the Tannadice stands and the team came out and did two encores.

LAURA HIRD: I had a flat in McLeod Street, Gorgie, and the day after Hearts won the Cup and brought it back to Gorgie I had a bit of a bad incident. The team came along Princes Street on the bus and they were heading for the ground and there were just tens of thousands of people in Gorgie from early in the morning, sitting on the rooftops and up on the railway bridge and on top of the bus stops. My dad had just missed it because he had died three months before Hearts had finally won the Cup and I was in a top-floor flat and I was wondering what to do when the team went past. So I thought I would tear up paper and when the bus comes under the bridge I'll throw the paper out of the window like confetti, and I was sat there for two hours tearing up all this paper and putting it in the biggest saucepan I could find. The bus came down McLeod Street and there were packed crowds below and I got hold of the saucepan to throw the paper. But my ring caught on the side of the pan and the whole lot went out, paper, saucepan and all. Down three floors straight into the crowd. My whole life flashed in front of me and I just got down on the floor and hid out of sight. Eventually I looked out of the window and there was a young girl rubbing her head. I decided the best thing to do was give myself up to the police and I went down and the girl said, 'It hit a man and then it hit me.' The man had already gone into the ground so I told the police if anyone collapses, it was me! I didn't dare go out of the house for the next three days and eventually I ventured out to The Tynecastle Arms thinking the fuss had all died down. But then a girl came up to me and said, 'You're the lass who threw the saucepan, we've got it on video!' I kept watching the papers in case someone had delayed concussion. It certainly put a damper on the celebrations.

BOB CRAMPSEY: I thought the situation of the last day of the 2002–03 season, where Celtic gradually saw things slipping away from them, was far more gripping than the Champions League final, which was technically admirable, some of the angles of the passing were spectacular but there was a certain sterility about it; not so much 'I will do something clever' and rather 'I will stop you doing anything at all'.

PETER DONALD: It's part of being an administrator, but most of my relationships are with the suits: the elected members, the politicians of football. The coaches and the managers look after the players. And it's not a situation when you can go out and have a drink with them at night, because there has to be a line. If the media see the SFA officials having a jolly old time it makes us a soft target. A classic example of that was when prior to the Mexico World Cup we went to Santa Fe in New Mexico to do acclimatisation. It was hard work for the players training every day at Santa Fe State College and I was there and other people were there doing their job and so on and a wee bit up the road was the Grand Canyon. Now that's pretty special and we had to miss the chance to see it because we couldn't be seen to have a jolly when we were there to do our work. In Mexico we stayed in Teotihuacan, which translated means 'the place where men become gods', and it was right beside two Aztec or Inca pyramids, in the middle of nowhere outside Mexico City. We stayed in this hotel and, I'm not kidding you, it was from here to those houses and I stayed there for three weeks and never had time to go and see them. Now people don't understand that. But the players are there working and you're there working, the only time you have is usually when it's dark. But that's your job.

BOB CRAMPSEY: The Real v. Eintracht match in 1960 was a brilliant, brilliant game, one of these great exercises of mass catharsis. It was a lovely night, but it didn't sell out. There were 127,000 at Hampden and it could hold 134,000. Eintracht scored first, which was no surprise at all because Eintracht had just taken 12 goals off Rangers, so the attitude was that they must be the best side in the world. Everyone there thought so. By half-time it was 3–1 and you could see the realisation spreading that, no, Eintracht were not the best side in the world. Then an outbreak of collective honesty that we had a long, long way to go to be as good as Eintracht even. To show you how naive people were in those days, for years and years STV didn't have a master tape of that match. They had taped six *Late Calls* over it in a fit of economy. The referee, Jack Mowat's, expenses for that match were sixpence, for the bus from his home to Hampden.

GORDON SHERRY: The 1997 Cup final is the game that stands out, and one of the few matches my mum ever went to. Not just the game because the game is a blur really – Paul Wright scoring in the eighth minute or something. It was just amazing. Whether Kilmarnock will ever win the Cup or the League again in my lifetime, I just don't know. The last time they won the cup was in 1929! But that day was something I'll never forget. The bus came up John Finnie Street and there were 30,000 people there. It may not mean much to someone not from Kilmarnock, but to witness that and be part of it was amazing. You could not move in any of the bars that night.

IAN WILSON: In Turkey I was with Besiktas, one of the top sides there, and the Turkish equivalent of Arsenal or Manchester United. The fans treat you well – if you won. They are fanatics

City rivals forever: Hibs v. Hearts derby of 1969. (© SNS Group)

over there, their passion is unbelievable. It can get out of hand but it's the most important thing in their lives. Football is top of the tree. In the two years I was out there, we did the Double twice.

ERIC MILLIGAN: I was taken to Tynecastle before I went to school and you would start to queue at 12.30 for a 3 p.m. kick-off. The kids were always at the front with their legs dangling over the dirt track and I doubt if that would be allowed now and dad would say, you stay there and don't move, and when the chocolate boy comes round I will buy you some chocolate, and he would go a few rows back and stand with my uncles. One of my first games was an Edinburgh derby and that's a game Hearts and Hibs supporters who were there will never forget. Davie Mackay was playing for Hearts, who were romping the league by scoring 132 goals to win the league with maximum goals and maximum points ever in the First Division of the Scottish League. They played Hibs in the Scottish Cup and were beaten 4–3. Joe Baker became a legend for Hibs fans because he scored all four goals. Now Joe was a great player and a great guy and I see him now and tease him a bit about that match, but on that occasion he didn't exactly please me. I remember looking at the Hibs fans and saying: 'So that's what Hibs supporters look like.' I had never seen guys so happy. Funnily enough, while I would put on a maroon scarf to go and watch the Hearts, it was by no means unusual if they were away for my dad to take me to Hibs and cheer on Joe Baker and the other Edinburgh team if they were playing someone like Rangers or St Johnstone. And he would put a green scarf round my neck! My dad thought there was nothing untoward about that and it wasn't unusual to find Edinburgh folk going to Hearts one weekend and the Hibs next, rather than travelling somewhere.

In terms of great occasions, you would always remember Europe, Standard Liège, Benfica, Real Zaragoza; in more recent times tussles with Hamburg and one famous occasion when they beat Bayern Munich 1–0 at Tynecastle. For sheer pleasure there was a challenge match against Torpedo Moscow, who I think were the Russian navy team. They played three Scottish sides. They beat Rangers and got a draw with Kilmarnock, which everyone thought was a fantastic result for Kilmarnock, and then they came to Tynecastle and Hearts beat them 6–0. Willie Hamilton, who only played for Hearts for a year or two before he was transferred to Hibs and then to Aston Villa, is a supremely gifted footballer who is almost forgotten in Scottish football. But for those short years he graced Tynecastle and Easter Road, he was unsurpassed by anybody.

ALEX TOTTEN: We were playing Falkirk and Simon Stainrod was playing for them and it had just gone to 1–1. At the restart Simon said to Kevin McAllister: 'I can see the goalkeeper off the line, just tip the ball slowly,' and he hit this ball from halfway and it just flew into the net and they beat us 2–1. Everyone was talking about this goal and the BBC and STV phoned us because I kept a tape of every home game. I told them there was no way they were getting the tape because every Saturday night it would be shown and show my goalkeeper being made a fool of. So I came home and I taped John Wayne over the top of it. It wasn't that good a goal anyway!

STUART COSGROVE: The other Dundee game that sticks in my mind – and I could talk about Dundee games all day – the one where we beat them 1–0 to go into Europe and just before we scored our goalkeeper, Alan Main, had an absolute stonewall save that kept us in the game and we went up the other end and scored and that put us into Europe. That was a huge, huge day for Saints, but it sticks in my memory for another reason; at half-time I was invited on the pitch to present the SPL Under-21 trophy, the first ever, decided the week before St Johnstone had won it, beating Celtic at Barrowfield, and I was presenting it to Marco McCulloch, our young left-back, and we were able to hold the trophy aloft to the Saints fans. The man who was co-presenting it with me was the then-chief executive of the SPL, Roger Mitchell, who had been involved in a lot of disputes with Dundee fans about whether or not their ground was suitable to let them in the Premier League or not and he was roundly booed and I was roundly booed because we were the two people who most represented anti-Dundeeism. The thought of holding up an SPL trophy won by St Johnstone in front of Dundee fans was just fantastic. You won't get many better days than that.

JOHN HUGHES: What turns me on is that sort of adrenalin rush before the game, knowing that you're going out to put a shift in. The same with the training – I just love to go in and train. There were times last year when I had to come off the grass because of my back. I've got a disc problem and it's really painful at times. I was going to try and get it operated on, but I cut my training instead and I had to sort of start playing the game in a different way. The disc comes out and it hits the nerves and it puts my muscles into spasm, but I took painkillers every Saturday and the anti-inflammatories. It won't stop me. No way. Nothing will.

4

THE BOSS

LAWRIE REILLY: Willie McCartney was manager when I signed for Hibs and he died early on in my career. In those days the managers died of old age, they never got sacked.

ALEX SMITH: Like everyone else I have taken a few dunts in that time. I was first-ever Stenhousemuir manager and learned how to run a club on a shoestring. There was 11 on the board so there was a six and five situation and you learned how to handle the political side of the boardroom. The president at the time, Peter Cowan, is a lovely man. A lovely wit and humour. He would phone me on a Monday afternoon and ask if I had half an hour spare to nip down and see him because some of the committee were gunning for me because I was using bad language in the dressing-room. He always prepared you for it.

It was a good grounding and they were a smashing wee club Stenhousemuir and an example to other clubs on how to keep a business within budget.

When I took over the committee had put their whole savings in to keep the club going.

I had made reference to not being good enough for Stenhousemuir to put the flag up and sign players on monthly contracts now and I insisted we had to get away from that.

The whole committee stood up and demanded an apology and I wouldn't. I couldn't see what I had said.

Mr Cowan said I had to apologise and once I had apologised he would explain why I was in the wrong. So I did and then the chairman told me everyone had been asked the year before to put money in the club to save it. Now, they were all working men and every single man put in what they had. In 1969, £500 was a fortune and some of them were putting in £1,500 or £2,000 to see the club to the end of the season. And they survived and we went from strength to strength and even went on and beat Rangers at Ibrox.

They were great times and you were allowed to learn the game and learn the job.

ALEX TOTTEN: I did better in management than I ever did as a player. I got Alloa promotion and after two years we were sitting sixth in the First Division. Falkirk were bottom when they came for me. Some said I was taking a chance, but I thought it was the opportunity to manage the club I supported as a kid. In November 1982 they were bottom and a year later they were sitting second top. Then on 11 November 1983, at eight o'clock in the morning, my wife says there's someone on the phone for you and this voice says: 'Jock Wallace here, son, how would you like to come to Rangers as my assistant?' I couldn't believe it. We played Clyde that day and Craigie Brown was manager and the Falkirk chairman told me Motherwell wanted to talk to me about the job there because Jock Wallace had left them to go to Rangers. I spoke to them at Coatbridge, they offered me a five-year contract because they had had so many managers and wanted continuity and the money was great. This was Monday night and I phoned them on the Wednesday to tell them I was turning it down and on the Friday I am at Ibrox going up the marble staircase and Big Jock is there to meet me. On the

Saturday we played Dundee United and Jock said: 'Come on, we'll go out on the field.' I couldn't believe it.

ALEX SMITH: My first manager was Willie Waddell at Kilmarnock. I was only there for a season because I was living in Stirling and the travelling was killing me. I was earning more in expenses than I was in wages.

But Kilmarnock were also going full-time and my father, like a lot of fathers of players at that time, wouldn't let me go full-time until I had finished my trade, which was in the glass trade.

There was no such thing as a tracksuit manager then. Jock Stein and Eddie Turnbull were probably the first. Before that the manager tended to pick the teams and the trainer took the training. The manager stood aloof from all that and there was an important gap between him and players. Captains tended to be very influential.

Scott Symon was probably the last of those sort of managers. When you met these men you were in awe of them. They all had the same quality; they were humble. It didn't matter how much success they had achieved they remained ordinary.

IAN WILSON: Jock Wallace's bark was worse than his bite. If you gave him 100 per cent he would give you 200 per cent back. He helped me settle into a house in Leicester and I was getting married at the time. When we were looking for furniture, he pointed me in the right direction. Jock was a big help for me early on. But he was a perfect gentleman. He did shout and scream occasionally but he was a big softie at heart. Jock took us out of the Second Division and into the First and into the semi-finals of the FA Cup.

ALEX TOTTEN: I was tipped to take over as team manager, but Rangers had a policy that every player got paid the same and some started leaving. Jimmy Nicholl left, John McLelland went to Watford – Watford from Rangers! Robert Prytz left as well.

What happened was Jock got the sack and Graeme Souness took over and the chairman then was a guy called Davie Holmes and he said: 'I want you to come and meet Graeme.'

So I went up to the Blue Room and there's Graeme Souness and he says: 'Can you introduce me to the players, Alex?' So I introduced them: Derek Johnstone, Peter McCloy, Ally Dawson, Davie Cooper, McCoist and that. But I knew I was leaving because I was Big Jock's man and everyone wants their own men. So Campbell Ogilvie took me round to see David Holmes and I was sacked by Rangers. It was a clean sweep and his first two signings were Chris Woods and Terry Butcher, the England goalkeeper and the England captain. Big Jock had spent maybe £600,000 in three years and Souness spent £16 million in three years.

ALEX SMITH: When I was sacked by St Mirren I had the chance of going to Rangers in charge of the youth set-up under Graeme Souness and Walter Smith. But Aberdeen had offered me the opportunity to work with first-team players and when I walked in the dressing-room they were basically all internationals: Willie Miller, Alex McLeish, Jim Bett, Stewart McKimmie, Charlie Nicholas, David Robertson, John Hewitt, Davie Dodds. So that was another management skill to be learned. I think they took to me very well. Willie and Alex had phoned me the week before asking me to take the job as they wanted someone of the mould of Alex Ferguson to come back and take over. It was a great honour to go there. The first year we lost to Rangers in a classic League Cup final and came second in the league. The following year we won the two cups and in 1990–91 we lost the league on the last day of the season at Ibrox. We had taken 23 points out of 24 and with five games to go no one believed we could do it. Rangers had lost 3–0 to Motherwell the week before and that third goal meant we could draw at Ibrox to win the league. I wanted to go there and win, but that complicated matters a bit. It was one of those days in football that will live with you forever and the fact we played 4–4–2 caused a lot of criticism. As a manager I had to carry the can and accept it, but I thought getting where we did was a feat in itself.

ALEX McLEISH: Alex Smith came in at a time when morale was quite low. Ian Porterfield was a decent bloke, but somehow didn't get the breaks. We were in a couple of Cup finals, but didn't get the sort of luck that sometimes goes with these games. As a result, we lost a bit of confidence and a bit of form. With Alex we won two trophies and came close to winning a Championship, as everyone from that era will remember. A draw at Ibrox would have done; whether going there for the win would have resulted in a different outcome we will never know. But we had our chances at 0–0 and it was one of those games you felt whoever got the first goal would win the game. But we did very well to come back from 20 points behind and time is a quick healer. The best way to learn is through your mistakes and if you can't do that you will never get out of the humdrum existence.

WILLIE YOUNG: You have a ringside seat and as long as you don't do anything stupid it's a marvellous ringside seat. I've had an Edinburgh Derby where all 22 players have shaken my hand at the end. When you are new to the game the stick you can get from managers can be difficult because they are not trying to influence you for that game; they are trying to influence you for the next one. I did Falkirk against Rangers and I chalked off a goal for Falkirk that would have given them a draw and Jim Jefferies was sat in the dugout raging about it. The following morning the papers said: 'Jefferies in ref rage'. In the afternoon STV showed the match and it showed the foul that led me to chalk off the goal, so I had been right. The following week I had Falkirk again and I was out inspecting the pitch when I saw Jim racing over and I knew what was coming: 'Willie, I just want you to know that I never said what that paper said I said.'

And I said: 'Jim, are you telling me this because you have a

conscience about it or because I am refereeing *your* game today?'
I have lots of run-ins with Jim Jefferies, but over that period I
think he has come to respect me.

JOHN LAMBIE: I try to put fun back into the game; players
should be looking forward to coming into training. This serious
stuff is no good to me because you don't get the best out of
people. I know there's time when you have to be serious but
there'd always time for a bit of laughter in the game.

That documentary on me and Partick Thistle: it won a gold
award down in London, but I didn't know half the things they
were doing. I didn't know they were taping what was going on in
the dressing-room at Clyde. And, of course, I'm effing and
blinding away. That guy from the TV company made fortunes
out of it; me and Gerry Collins shared £1,000. Don't get me
wrong, there were times, like in the dugout, when I knew I was
wired up, but you forget that in a game. You forget all about it.
The head man came and said they would cut a lot of it, but then
they decided later they couldn't cut anything, because it's good
television. I'm a Christian at heart – my daughters go to church
– and I said: 'Christ, you'll get me crucified for this!' The club
gave permission, but I wasn't too happy.

It is what happens in the game and it's realistic and there was
no con stuff in it. I forgot about the cameras half the time. I've
done another film. It's a personal one of the last four games with
Partick and it was done by the people who do the match videos.
But that's not going out, or at least I hope it's not.

All the stress has given me shingles and that's why I'm suffering
right now. The doctor says to me, 'You've nae chance of a heart attack
because you let it all out. It's the boys who keep it in who you have to
worry about.' I just cannae help myself. There's times when I've
promised I would go out and stay quiet. I've been up to the directors'
box to watch the game from there, but you wouldn't count to 20
before I was back down in the dugout. Oh, I couldn't stand that. I'm

one of these guys who have to kick every ball with my players.

I've seen more of my grandkids Stephanie and Melissa since I stepped down. I've three daughters and two granddaughters. I can't seem to get a male to come into the line.

I am going away on a cruise for 13 days, which is something I could never have done till I got out. The club have been great to me. They gave me a testimonial, which was a sell-out, and it's been good. Forty-three years in the game is a long time to wait to pick up a few bob because one thing's for sure, I never made any money when I was in it. I packed up a good business to come into football. I was a bookmaker and was even doing that part-time when I was coaching with Hibs. I worked at the dog tracks and the Epsom Derby.

I turned down the Hamilton job three times and I couldn't believe it when they came back again. I turned them down first time because they just wanted me to take it to the end of the season. Bertie Auld was manager at that time. Eventually I took it and sold off my betting shops – so I went from no stress to plenty of stress.

ALEX TOTTEN: I went to Dumbarton and then St Johnstone. I never got a crowd at Dumbarton because they all got on the bus across Erskine Bridge to Ibrox and Parkhead and that's why I left. At St Johnstone we went from the Second Division to the Premier League in three years, and played in three semi-finals of the Cup. I loved St Johnstone. We had had one defeat in eight games, were lying seventh in the Premier League, had played Rangers at Hampden in the Skol Cup and Geoff Brown came in and said he wanted to make a few changes; so I got the sack from there. Everyone was astounded because it came right out of the blue.

I think Geoff thought we are out in the sticks and no one would take much notice but there were three pages on it in every newspaper. When I got home Chic Young was there with the cameras and I got 400 letters from all over Scotland. Big Aggie the tea lady gave me a cake saying, 'There's only one Alex Totten', which I showed to the Browns. I don't think they were too happy.

I went to East Fife, got them promotion, then Kilmarnock came for me and I took over from Tommy Burns, which wasn't easy because Tommy was a very popular guy. I was there two and a half years, saw the stands go up to make it an 18,000 all-seater stadium and got sacked by them in December – it's not been a great month for me, December! – and three days later George Fulsom came in for us at Falkirk. Five months later I took Falkirk to the Cup final to play Kilmarnock.

Their manager was Bobby Williamson and when I got the sack Bobby, who comes from Easterhouse and is a real hardie, had tears coming down his face. Bobby got the job as reserve-team coach at Rangers on my recommendation and we were very close.

So there we were at Hampden, walking our teams out, and I had signed seven of their players so it was a funny feeling. I wore a kilt and Jock Bown was my lawyer and was also commentating on TV, and he had told me that when we walked out he was going to say, 'And Alex Totten was resplendent in the Falkirk tartan,' which he did, of course.

The feeling of beating Celtic in the semi-final and getting to the final was incredible. Kevin McGrillen scored, Celtic must have had 22 corners and I was praying for Willie Young to blow the final whistle. On the way back we stopped at The Roman Bar at Camelon; this was about 10.30 p.m. and when I left at 6 the next morning wee Kevin McAllister was still there with his mother and his wife. We'd beaten a team that had Di Canio, Cadete and Andreas Thom in it.

STV and Sky gave me a tape of the final and I've never watched it.

It's inevitable that one day you are going to get the sack. Fergie was sacked at St Mirren; Alf Ramsey won the World Cup and he was sacked.

ALEX SMITH: You need a thick skin in this business. As a player you get dropped, you get signed by teams and you get released by teams. As a manager you have to be tough because it is inevitable that you will get a dunt. It's how you handle that that matters. If you handle it with decorum and dignity you can usually go and get another position. You bounce back, in other words.

STUART COSGROVE: They described Paul Sturrock's illness as a heart attack but it was an anxiety attack. His body was seizing up with too much stress. I was talking to him recently on the phone, and it's odd. He was saying one of the things he doesn't understand about Scotland and the Scottish football press is that when he was manager at St Johnstone he was under day-to-day pressure from the media, whereas in Plymouth the only paper that is remotely interested in what's going on there is the guy from the local evening paper. They meet up once a week for a beer, Sturrock gives him his team thoughts and the guy goes away with his nice little exclusive. The nearest other club is 350 miles away. Whereas in Scotland there are so many papers all looking for different angles and they are not interested in St Johnstone, they are interested in the fact that Aggie Moffat, our tea lady, has thrown a kettle at Graeme Souness.

Those were great days because we had this wee war going with Rangers because Walter Smith and Alex Totten, our boss at the time, were involved in a punch-up in the tunnel and it ended in court. Once it all calmed down the arresting police officer said: 'I will bail you, but you have to go away from the ground,' and they ended up in one of the director's houses where they were getting reports from the game every ten minutes phoned through to them. So they actually sat and watched the television as mates. I was talking to Walter recently and he said: 'I don't know what I was thinking about, but at the time the game's the most important thing in the world.'

ALLAN GRIEVE: We've had amazing characters. The club's first manager, which was really before my time, was Tom Ferguson. He founded the club, he was Stirling Albion, it was his club. He was a local coal merchant, businessman and he put the money up to start

181

Stirling Albion and from 1945 through to the mid '60s he ran the club in every aspect. He occasionally did employ a manager or a coach but they seldom stayed very long because Tom just wanted to do it all himself. More recently Alex Smith was our manager for a long period from 1974 through to 1986, before he went off to look after St Mirren and Aberdeen and so on. Alex had 12 years at Stirling Albion, which is a long time for a manager at any level in Scottish football, and then more recently we had a short spell of six months when Jim Cleeton was our manager – a hugely successful spell. Then John Brogan, Kevin Drinkell and Ray Stewart managed for periods with varying degrees of success.

ARTHUR MONTFORD: Jock Stein and Willie Waddell, who was a great Rangers manager, both enjoyed European success: the Cup-Winners' Cup with Rangers a few years after Celtic had won in Lisbon. They spent some time in the '60s going over to Italy studying the Italian techniques, training, diet stuff like that and they both learned a lot. The players here didn't know anything about the value of pasta, fruit and other foods on the day of a game. Training technique had been four or five laps round the ground, kick the ball around and that was that.

ALEX SMITH: Being pals with Billy Bremner who played with Leeds and Dave Catenach who was with Celtic helped me in management because it meant I was able to get into the inner sanctums of both clubs.

When Don Revie took over at Leeds, Billy was just getting established and I would go down there for two or three days at a time and I was mixing with the likes of Norman Hunter, Terry Cooper and Paul Madeley. I was privy to a lot of how Revie operated. Up here with Davie Catenach, there would be George Connolly, Davie Hay, Kenny Dalglish even. I was getting information on how things were run. I got to know Jock Stein and his wife Jean very well and I could ring him and ask advice any time.

Eddie Turnbull was ahead of his time. He set the platform at Aberdeen and probably Alex Ferguson got the benefit of that. The structure was put in place by Eddie. He was an excellent coach and never reaped the benefits at Pittodrie because Hibs came back in for him.

I remember going to a meeting at Bridge of Allan called by Hal Stewart, the ex-Morton supremo. It was a crisis meeting because crowds were going down and it was probably the start of the move to get three or four divisions instead of the old two. It was a three-day seminar and the managers that were there included Jock Stein, Eddie Turnbull, Willie Waddell, Bob Shankly, Bobby Ansell. All the top managers were there. I sat there and never opened my mouth; I just sat and listened.

CRAIG LEVEIN: I had this great plan of playing till I was 35; I was very fit (not like I am now) and I just envisaged I would play till I was 35. I always fancied going to Australia, taking my family with me, and playing or coaching, but obviously I was in the position where I hadn't played long enough to do that. I wanted to coach, that was what I wanted to do, but it was just forced upon me a little bit earlier than I would have liked. I worked hard at coaching as I had at playing. I've got a root fear of not being successful, whatever I do. That was what was good about Cowdenbeath. I made a lot of mistakes and was able to correct the mistakes without anybody really knowing what had happened. I learned about the way I dealt with players, getting the best out of players individually and as a team – all the things that go into making a good coach. I made mistakes at them all and I've learned from them. I'm sure there's a hell of a lot more mistakes to come. The weird thing was that we would progress. We got better as the years went on at Cowdenbeath. All of which enabled me to eventually take up this job. It's a difficult game, you have to keep improving, keep getting better. When you stand still that's when everybody else catches up with you.

DAVID McGREGOR: We came from the depths of despair in the early '70s when we went one season where we won only one game. There were a couple of guys, Sam Smith and Gordon Webster, who took the club by the scruff of the neck in about 1975 and within three years we were playing a Cup semi-final at Hampden. They brought in Archie Knox who had played with the club as a schoolboy, then moved to St Mirren and Dundee United. He came as manager in '76, which was the start of a career that saw him become manager at Man United, Rangers, Everton and Scotland and who could ever have dreamed of that for a lad who was born on a farm just outside Forfar.

BOB CRAMPSEY: A quiz question: Busby, Stein, Shankly – how many caps between them? The answer is seven and Shankly had six of them, Stein none at all. My theory is that the great managers have been serviceable, run-of-the-mill players. Ferguson is another case in point. Dalglish is an apparent contradiction to that, but the groundwork at Liverpool had been done before and really it was like a new general manager coming in to take over Marks and Sparks.

JIM LEISHMAN: My first coaching job was Oakley, then I went to Kelty Hearts and was then head-hunted by Cowdenbeath where Andy Rolland, ex-Dundee United, was the manager at the time. After three or four months Andy resigned and that was me, I went back to Kelty then got the youth job under Pat Stanton in 1980.

Managers, George Miller, Alex Wright and Willie McLean, his assistant, all helped me. Alex Smith was always available for advice, but then you do your own thing. My own thing was to be myself. I didn't say I was a great tactician and I didn't say I was a great coach, but I like to think I was a fair man-manager. Initially with the poems and all that it was great fun, but I think I got a kick in the balls for that because people didn't see the serious side to the football. They just thought 'he laughs and jokes', but sometimes you need that. Certainly when I took over Dunfermline bottom of the Second Division, they needed a laugh and a joke.

ALEX TOTTEN: A manager has to be a mother, father, psychiatrist and psychologist because the players come in with all their woes. Some you kick, some you cuddle. You have to be prepared to deal with everything. Our physio, Bob McCallum, who I was very close to, died as we were preparing for the Cup final and I had to speak at his funeral. We had to deal with provisional liquidation at Falkirk, too. The players were told on the Friday that there were no wages and the next day they went to St Mirren and won 2–0. At one time I thought the key was going in the door and there would be no more Falkirk Football Club.

Football is like a jigsaw – a blend of youth and experience. Respect has to be earned and I am keen on discipline; I don't allow jeans or anything like that and the players have to be on time. I signed John Henry, who is now with Falkirk, for Kilmarnock and we were playing Celtic at Rugby Park. I was due to name the team at 2 p.m. and John came in puffing and panting at ten-past and said: 'Sorry, gaffer, I got stuck in the Clyde tunnel,' and I said, 'I don't give a monkey's. You're not playing.' He was never late again.

If anyone mucks about they are out the door. You have to set the example. In five and a half years at St Johnstone I never had a day off, so you have to be conscientious, too.

Everywhere I've been, even at the three clubs I got the sack from, I've always been very welcome. A while back I was offered money by newspapers to tell the story about St Johnstone, but I refused.

Bert Paton always points out that I was the club comic when I was playing and now I am deadly serious, so maybe it's not as much fun. I was born in a single end – gas mantles, toilet outside – and that's when you appreciate things. Now maybe we spoil the kids and they don't have to work for anything.

JIM LEISHMAN: I have been involved in a few scrapes with players and you don't survive unless you have got a nasty streak as well. When it comes to letting them go you look at the player and say: 'Time up.' Firstly, it's for your benefit and secondly, if he's a young lad who is not going to progress here it's time to move on. If it's a senior pro and he's no good for the team you are making the decision for the good of the team. So there are ways that you can focus, so it's not hurting as much. Sometimes it's harder to tell a youngster but other times it's not, because you are being honest to the youngster and say you are going to have to make progress somewhere else.

It's not nice when you see a young kid crying or an old guy crying because his time is up, especially if they've enjoyed it, but to progress you have to move on. They've seen me crying, too, because that's football and I am an emotional person. As for the headbangers, I just say if you don't want to come on board, fair enough. The bus is waiting, jump on, or get off and stay off.

My rewards are I've won five Championships, I've been BELL'S Manager of the Year; money you can spend easy, memories you can keep forever. There are too many memories and they've gone too quickly at times. You don't have time to appreciate them. There are a lot of similarities between Dunfermline and Livingston because they were in the bottom league when I took over and they went up the way, third, second, first. Again, it was a team effort: Davie Hay, Raymond Stewart, Ian Miller, Alan Preston, John Robertson, George McNeil, Mike Karaopvic, Peter the Kitman, Danny the Kitman, everybody. My first game at Dunfermline there were 697 people against Queen of the South. The supporters had left and we had to build it up again. We beat them 1–0 with a Davie Wilcox header and I can remember the goal as if it was yesterday. But 697, it was a tragedy. I was at the game when Celtic had won the League and Dunfermline had won the Cup and the League game was on the Tuesday. You couldn't get in. There were two deaths, someone fell off the stand and there was a crash with the floodlights. The official capacity was 26,000 at the time, but there must have been 30,000 in there. Unbelievable. I'm sitting there as a young player making my way and three years later you're out there.

I took it from 697 to averaging 10,000 and 4,500 people walked up Dunfermline High Street in protest when I left. But there is no bitterness – it's too short a life.

ALLAN GRIEVE: Kevin Drinkell is quite simply the best manager of all the ones that I've worked with – absolutely outstanding as a man-manager. He treated all the players as individuals, he knew their characters inside out, their strengths and weaknesses and was able to get the best out of players who had been deemed trouble-makers and failures elsewhere. An absolutely outstanding manager and in my time with Stirling Albion the decision the club made to part company with Kevin in 1998 was the worst decision they ever made. He had a short spell as manager of Montrose and after that he's just really been involved as an agent.

Leader of men: Kevin Drinkell was outstanding at Stirling Albion. (Photo courtesy of Allan Grieve)

Kevin, in fact, still lives in Stirling and attends probably about three-quarters of Stirling Albion matches, so he has the seat next to me in the stand and we reminisce about the great old days.

DAVID McGREGOR: We went up as Champions in 1983–84, winning promotion on the last Saturday in March and the League on the first Saturday in April and broke all the points records going that season. We only lost four games in the whole season. I often say that if you had Doug Houston, who is no longer in the game, as joint manager of a side with Archie Knox and had Archie's ruggedness and motivation alongside Doug's tactical awareness, you would have a fantastic management team. Once, at Stenhousemuir, we arrived and there was nobody there, the gates were still shut. We couldn't get into the dressing-room, but were desperate to see the pitch and, I always remember, Archie kicked the door in. The Stenhousemuir chairman went ballistic. The standing joke was that we didn't only employ a manager, we had to employ a joiner to repair all the dressing-room doors.

He was followed by Alex Rae, who had a great career in football, and Tommy Campbell in the '90s. Tommy was a very ebullient guy who, of course, created mayhem once he left for Arbroath. Tommy wouldn't mind me saying this, but he's a devout Catholic and apart from the fact he is now St Johnstone's youth development officer, he's also a great Celtic fan and he had this great thing about all the referees. He was convinced all the referees were masons. One night in a cricket club bar down in Prestwick, Louis Thau, the referee, handed me this envelope and said, 'Give that to Tommy when you get back to Forfar.' So I gave him it and he opened the envelope and this note read: 'How can Joseph John Timmins and Kevin O'Donnell be masons?' Tommy's reply would be unprintable! They were getting their own back at him.

IAN BLACK: We've even had Ally McLeod at Queen of the South, Bobby Shearer, Davie Wilson, the Rangers player. John Connolly is a very passionate guy. He is his own man and he's got his own ways of working, like anybody I suppose, but he's certainly good at bailing us out.

CHARLIE REID: Hibs made the mistake with Franck Sauzee; they should never have put him in as manager without a guy behind him

Fallen hero: Franck Sauzee was discarded by Hibs after a brief spell as manager.
(© *Daily Record*/Mirrorpix)

with experience. Or they should have put him in as an assistant manager and he would probably have still been here and taking them forward. It was very sad and I think every Hibs supporter feels bad for Franck over what happened.

Alex McLeish got some stick when he left Easter Road, but I would say to any Hibs supporter – and I am as rabid a Hibs fan as anyone anywhere – if you were offered a job with double the wage and seven or eight times the money to spend on players, you would have taken the job as well. A bigger job will beckon and that probably means English football. Maybe he will be offered the Scotland job, but is that bigger than Rangers these days?

JACK McCONNELL: I have a lot of time for Alex McLeish, who's an absolute credit to the game, and there are a lot of these guys around. It's interesting to see a lot of that '80s playing generation doing well. Craig Levein is another committed to the game, committed to young people and a very nice person. They will do the Scottish game well in the future.

Alex Smith has never had full credit for what he has achieved. He stayed with the same small club for a long time and produced a lot of good footballers and then went to other clubs, neither of which were Rangers or Celtic, and won the Scottish Cup with them. That is rarely done in any country and he did it in Scotland, which is a fantastic achievement. Men like that, who have mucked away in the Scottish game for 30 years or more, are the mainstay of the game here. They are the foundation on which the game is built.

I saw Alex recently and he has a youth apprentice scheme at Ross County going and he has youngsters coming from all over the Highlands, and from elsewhere, even Lanarkshire. They are living in digs in Dingwall, learning the trade, and learning it properly. He could easily go to Ross County, buy in a few cheap players or free transfers and try and stay in the First Division, but he is building a community club that is going to be a big success. And that is that commitment that is unique to sport; there are people out there who give that little bit extra and that's a fantastic thing in Scottish football. One of the benefits of being involved with Stirling Albion was that I met a lot of these guys and I have nothing but admiration for them.

LORD MACFARLANE: I said when he was at Cowdenbeath that Craig Levein looked like a super young manager and that he was going to be a manager of great class and of course he's already beginning to show that. I have a very good friend called Neil Watt, who played for Stranraer, and he has just gone back to manage them. He's a super young man, very good in business, and maybe 35 to 37 – just the right age. He is not dependent on Stranraer for his bread and butter, but he'll make a huge contribution. There are some very good young people beginning to come up through the ranks. Everybody knew that Alex McLeish should be a top manager, but of course you can never be certain, it would have been easier if it hadn't been Rangers. Their

The next generation: Craig Levein is rated one of the country's top managerial hopes.
(© *Daily Record*/Mirrorpix)

expectancy is so extraordinary that you're never quite sure, so in a way everybody in football is very pleased that he's made the grade, although he himself said he only needs to lose two weeks in succession and he's got a big problem.

TERRY CHRISTIE: Bob Shankly was no great football coach and the managers years ago tended not to be technically good coaches, but what he did do was he spoke with a player and he knew when players were playing well and he had the good sense not to interfere with something that was working well. What happened, the Dundee team, they actually operated a very sophisticated style of play, but Bob Shankly had never invented this sophisticated style of play. Gordon Smith played deep, Andy Penman inside on forward runs, the inside-left was Gilzean but he really played as a striker and the centre-forward dropped off in midfield. It was a really complex, very sophisticated way to play and Bob hadn't designed this. He had got all the ingredients, put them in the pot and the players all played to their strengths and Bob Shankly had the good sense to never interfere with it.

CRAIG BROWN: I worked for a wonderful manager at Rangers called Scott Symon – a genuine sort and a real gentleman. Integrity was his watchword. He was very dignified in everything he did, he had three years at Ibrox.

I was Bob Shankly's first signing when he was manger at Dundee and his last transfer out before he left, so my career at Dundee coincided exactly with Bob's. The great thing about these famous Scottish managers was their honesty – they were blunt to a fault. They spoke their mind and left you in no doubt that they were very, very straight and there was never any bitterness and I have tried to do that in football. You can't please everyone but you try to be fair and that was my overriding impression of Scott Symon and Bob Shankly. Bob wasn't a great tactician but where he excelled was in his eye for a player. He didn't make many signing errors and he had very good discipline. He was very hot on turn-out. We were the first team in Scotland to have round-necked jerseys and the exact amount of turnover on the socks. The jersey had to be inside the shorts; he was very tidy and organised in things like that and I took that from him. Bob had plenty of humour. He never called me 'Craig'; he always called me 'Christ, Craig' and even if I had the occasional good game he would say: 'Christ, Craig, that was a good game you had today!'

There was always that element of surprise in his voice. The phone would ring in the Dens dressing-room and someone would answer it and say: 'Boss, that's the press wanting the team,' and Bob would look round and say: 'Tell them our Greta hasnae picked it yet,' Greta being his wife of course.

I had three managers when I was playing at Falkirk: Alex McCrae, Sammy Kean and John Prentice. Terry Christie I rate as one of the best managers in Scotland. People have often asked me who was best and I always say: Terry Christie. The problem has been he was never prepared to go full-time.

There has never been a week in my life without football. I had a spell in part-time journalism at the *Dundee Courier,* when I was reporting matches, then I came back into the game as manager of Motherwell in 1974 and have been a manager or coach ever since. I don't know if there is a formula for managing players but I try and treat them all the same way, with a certain degree of respect and trust that they reciprocate and they will treat you similarly. I think it's only right you are respectful of colleagues.

I do think the hardest thing in football management is to release a player – the time when you have to say to a player: 'You are no use, you are not up to standard.' It's part of the job, but it is certainly not pleasant.

ALEX SMITH: I went to Stirling in 1974 and at the time Bob Shankly was general manager and sat on the board. I thought Jack the Lad was ready to manage any club, but I learned more in three months with Bob Shankly than I had done on my own in five years.

He had a wonderful sense of humour without realising it. The knowledge I picked up from Bob Shankly has stood me in great stead over the years.

There's a great story about Terry Christie when Bob was manager at Stirling Albion. Terry was making runs from right-half to outside-left and Bob was getting on to him at half-time: 'Look, Terry, when you make runs forward you in front of the outside-right or inside-right position or centre-forward. Don't come over the centre line. You will unbalance the team and they will attack us through the hole you are leaving. No buts, Terry.'

'But boss, Alan Ball does that.'

'You mean the Alan Ball who plays for England? Alan Ball can run wherever he wants to run. He's got 105 English caps. He's got a World Cup medal. He's Alan Ball. You are Terry Christie and you will run where I tell you to run!'

Bob, typical miner, could kill you with a one-liner. He hated players being injured. We had a boy at Stirling Albion called Robert Duffin. He was a bit of a lad, always trying to get the last word on Bob. Robert had been recovering from a dislocated shoulder and had been about five weeks in rehab. He's there in the corridor pressing his arms up against the wall and he turns round to Bob and says: 'You know, boss, I feel like Christ now, I feel like the Lord.'

And Bob says: 'Aye, you may feel like him, son. You may even look like him, but the difference is he was back among us in three days – it's six weeks gone by and there's no sign of you yet.'

GORDON BROWN: It is no coincidence that so many great Scottish managers came from the same background. It was partly the mining tradition of Scotland when people worked to get out of the mines and football was one of the ways out. There is also the Scottish ethic of hard work and determination that today Ferguson represents and in the past Busby, Shankly and Stein did. I had the privilege to meet Jock Stein and he was a great man fired with the same sense of determination. When I read Ferguson's views on it he put it down to hard work, but of course it is also leadership skills and all the great players and managers have possessed those.

I have had over the years the chance to meet some of the country's great managers. I met Ferguson before his departure to Old Trafford when he was still the toast of Scotland for his feats with Aberdeen during the '80s. He struck me at once as a man who had never lost touch with his roots in Govan. He gave me the impression that no matter how high he climbed his feet would remain firmly on the ground.

Andy Roxburgh was different in his approach and I always thought that as a former teacher he brought useful skills to the management of our more volatile international players. Perhaps his greatest achievement was to lower the expectations of the Scottish football public to a level more in keeping with our small population and our status in the football world.

DAVID McGREGOR: I've never personally had to sack anyone. I took over when Ian McPhee had gone and I would never have sacked Ian McPhee. I would have rather resigned myself because he's my best mate in football, and still is, but he always said he would know when he'd had enough. There was one of our games, a midweek game at the end of the season, and we had three ex-managers – Tommy Campbell, Neale Cooper and Ian McPhee – in our boardroom at the game and another chairman who was there said: 'You must have a great club. Our ex-managers are still trying to sue me and here all yours are having a drink with you. You'll have to tell me how you do this.'

TERRY CHRISTIE: Bob gave us a pre-season talk and gave us some of his philosophy in life, which was really about retaliating first; you do it to them before they do it to you. He had had a hard life, Bob Shankly, and he believed everything was achieved by hard work. If you played for Bob Shankly you knew you had to work hard. He could be quite funny, but he didn't have the lighter side.

Bob had one joke. If you won a match and you were getting ready and maybe having your cup of tea and Bob was happy you'd won a game, he would say: 'As the late Willie McCartney used to say, "Let's get to hell out of here."' Now Willie McCartney was a famous man who was manager of the Hibs and when Bob told that story you knew that he was ecstatically happy about winning the game. Bob Shankly was a great influence on Alex Smith because he was a wise man, Bob Shankly. He was a great one for looking at the players as they came in to the ground on a Saturday and Bob really believed that if your head was down and you weren't smiling he wasn't that keen on playing you. The players learnt this so we all walked head high. He would stand there, with his suit on and trousers tucked into his socks, and a pair of football boots.

Bob, although I pictured him as a sort of gruff, growling guy, did have a softer side and he was very appreciative of the fact that I was doing two things. He had a Scots respect for learning and he respected the fact that I was at university. Alan Gilzean and Alan Cousin also taught.

BRIAN FLYNN: I think Alex Ferguson has the same affection for this neck of the woods, obviously for Rangers big time, but, you know, you can chart his history through Falkirk as a player and a manager. At any time, if we're doing any fund-raising for the club and you ask him to send something up, he's got no hesitation whatsoever in getting a playing strip to sign. You just can't buy that sort of thing it's fantastic.

TERRY CHRISTIE: I always wanted to be a manager. I always knew I was going to be a schoolteacher, so I really started when I was 23 by running school teams. I was realistic enough to know that I was nothing special as a player. Compared to the normal guy walking the street I was, but compared to the real players I wasn't good.

BRIAN FLYNN: Alex Totten is one of the good guys. He has a sort of razor-sharp sense of humour and he'll catch you out now and again just with one of his one-liners or one of his jokes. He is the old-fashioned Alex Ferguson-type of manager – very strict and a disciplinarian in his time. In his last spell as manager it was all financial and he lost a lot of experienced players. He had to play with kids and struggled badly in the season before last, but he has a great football brain and is a great motivator, terrific at getting players going. He has had run-ins and tussles with referees, but once the game's over, it's shake hands and make friends; he can bollock you one minute and be a pal the next. You've got to have that as a manager, you can't allow petty arguments in the dressing-room to cloud how you feel about somebody, and I think he's always been like that. He's always been, 'If you give me 100 per cent and you've got some ability and you don't mess me about you know you've got a chance.'

He left here to go as assistant to Jock Wallace when Jock took the management job at Rangers and that was just before the Souness era, but I have a lot of time for him. I've played golf a few times with him and he's a wily, wily, very dour competitor. He gets down on himself if he's not playing well and you know he can be bad company on the golf course if that's the case because he's muttering to himself and complaining.

Yogi Hughes is a Hibs man, but for some reason he has a real affection for this club and I think that would be what carries him through any failings that he has as a manager. He has enthusiasm for the club, for the game, and his knowledge of the type of player that he wants to come here and take the club to the next stage. John Collins was one of his first phone calls, I believe. His contract with Fulham was up and he made the call and said 'Would you like to come and play for us?' Obviously Collins said 'no', but at least he's setting his sights high.

TERRY CHRISTIE: I probably learned to be a manager at

Newtongrange Star. I've always been an organiser, looking at how things should be done – very critical – and I was eager to learn. Very early on in my managerial career at Meadowbank I inherited a team with a lot of tall guys and we became experts at set-pieces. One of the directors was unhappy with me because we were scoring so many goals from corner kicks and free kicks. He said, 'I'm bloody fed up with this.'

I had some tall guys and great kickers of the ball firing it in at great pace and big guys attacking and I had them all standing in the right places. Against Queen's Park within five minutes we had three corner kicks and we scored three goals. I get criticised for being over-defensive, but that's just because it's unusual for people to have a well-organised team. People are used to seeing teams that are not well organised, where you get maybe more goals than you get at these matches, but, no, I couldn't run a team that didn't play pass the football, it's just not fun.

When you let players go, you just do it from experience – you know it's not a pleasure but you've done it so often. You just say: 'I'm not offering you a new contract,' and people say it's worse for the young ones, but that's not true. It's far worse for the older ones. One of the things that makes a footballer a footballer is he's got to believe in himself, and at times it can get a wee bit personal. But I would say: 'I'm going to meet you in four or five years and we're going to be pals.' Footballers accept that the season comes to an end and you either get re-signed or you're out the door. There's an acceptance of that, there's an acceptance that the manager stands up at 2 p.m. and reads out the team and you're either in or out. If you give people bad news, you can't maybe argue with bad news, but everybody wants to kill the messenger. Telling players is just a matter of looking them in the eye and telling them. Some people say players have easy lives and Monday to Friday they do have an easy life, but in the blink of an eye it's over – you're 33, 34 and that's you finished.

DOUGRAY SCOTT: My twin girls, Gabriel and Edith, have been to Easter Road and we went to a game the season before between Hibs and Rangers, Alex McLeish's first game back at Easter Road since taking over Rangers. We are very good friends and I invited him to the *Mission Impossible 2* premiere and he came down and we sort of hit it off, we got on very well. His family were brought up in Barrhead and my dad's family were brought up in Barrhead as well, about three streets along from each other. The Dougrays are still there in Barrhead, so there's that connection, but we just got on well, very well. We are good buddies really and we see each other a lot and we've got a great passion for football, although he's got a bigger passion than I have. I wasn't surprised to see him go on and be such a success, because he was such a phenomenal manager for Hibs and you can tell instinctively. I'm very instinctive about football even though I'm an actor, and I know when someone's a good communicator. I'm really just a fan but I knew that he would go on to a bigger club; it was inevitable and he's done it – I mean five trophies in a year and a half. He's got great charisma. He's not old but he's in that old school. There are not many managers who can get away with the sort of man-management style of Alex Ferguson, but because he learned under Alex Ferguson for so many years and he has that kind of toughness about him and I think he commands the same kind of respect amongst his players that Ferguson gets from his players. He's very clever, Alex McLeish, he's very, very clever with the press as well, and incredibly passionate about football.

ALEX McLEISH: People compare me with Sir Alex, but I think we are different. There is no doubt that when you work with someone who is so successful you tend to take traits or ways of working from that person. We are similar in the way we are off the park and with our pals and that, but maybe different in the dressing-room. I was speaking to Sir Alex recently and I was asking him if he could do it in the same way with this current generation as he did way back

Alex Ferguson hugs Gordon Strachan after Aberdeen's Scottish Cup final
game against Celtic in 1984. Aberdeen won 2–1.
(© The Scotsman Publications Limited)

and he said: 'Absolutely not.' Things have moved on. These days there are agents. In those days if you didn't do it on the park you were out of the team; now there's psychology and you have to be a bit of everything. You have to evolve and I am sure Alex Ferguson would have evolved in any era.

RICHARD GORDON: For Gothenburg the ferry was all booked up so I had to fly, and it was the first time I had ever flown, but it was the chance to see my team take on Real Madrid in a European Cup final. I look back and I see videos and footage of the team at that time and it was a phenomenal team, but I took them totally and completely for granted at the time because I watched them every week and was used to them winning and it's only now you look back and see what Ferguson did with that bunch of guys – and some of those players who were in that team were by no means outstanding talents – but he got something out of them both individually and as

The Falkirk team line-up in 1970–71. Alex Totten is third from left, back row. Alex Ferguson far right, front row. (Photo courtesy of Alex Totten)

a collective. You look at what he did in Aberdeen with limited resources. Dougie Bell had been freed by St Mirren and within 18 months he's an absolutely mesmerising opponent in the European Cup semi-final – he did that with player after player. And the guys who were there, McLeish, Miller, Leighton, he gave them a mentality which they maintain to this very day, a winning mentality.

ALEX TOTTEN: When I came to Falkirk, Fergie was there, too, and to play for my home town team was great. Fergie then was just like he is now, the shop leader, the union man and it was clear even at Dunfermline and Falkirk that if anyone would make it as a manager it would be him. He was very determined and wanted to win. I used to travel with him every day and he was dogmatic and knew the game.

RICHARD GORDON: The only surprise for me was that it was Alex McLeish, rather than Willie Miller, who has been a major success in management because while Alex Ferguson was the leader and the winner, Willie was the leader of the team on the field and you always saw him as the driving force, as Fergie's man on the pitch. Willie will tell you he probably made a mistake going into management at Aberdeen at a time when things were rocky. The expectation levels were so high I think that if Willie had maybe done what Alex McLeish did and gone away and started elsewhere, he would have fared better.

Alex McLeish, I think, handles the job incredibly well. He plays the media perfectly. The thing he's got that other managers haven't is that he knows us, he knows what we need. He doesn't always give it to us obviously, but he's got an understanding and the relationship is there and he knows how to play us. When Rangers won the league, he addressed the crowds and it was like listening to the most consummate politician or orator that you had heard, because he said exactly the right things, he left pauses and he hit the buttons. Some people weren't convinced when he took the job and there he is now with them eating out of the palm of his hands. I was in night classes when he was there and it's great all these years later to see what he's done with himself. There's a lot of talk about Martin O'Neill being Manchester United manager at some time in the future, but my money would be on Alex McLeish.

CRAIG BROWN: There is a lovely quote in a book called *Football in Sunlight and Shadow*, it's written by a Uruguayan called Eduardo Galiano. He talks about South American football and it starts off with a marvellous quote: 'We lost, we won; either way we had fun.' I adapted that as a motto for the kids in Scotland. I have been fortunate in my life to have been involved in football in all aspects and one thing I have learned is that you have to have a few smiles along the way.

What you do is you do your best and you win some, you lose some and you take that quote into life. That quote you can put against me.

You need the skin of a rhinoceros if you are Scotland manager.

It is polarised in many ways; you go from lavish praise to horrendous abuse. One of the sportswriters, Bill Leckie, once said when we qualified for Euro '96 and then when we qualified for the World Cup '98: 'I would have Craig Brown's babies.' That's when we were doing OK, when you start to lose a couple of games you find out who your true friends are. I try never to get carried away with praise, so when they start criticising you can take it. Some of the expectation they have of you can be a bit unreasonable at times.

JOHN LAMBIE: I don't regret any of it. I signed for Falkirk in 1959 from Whitburn Juniors and I'm lucky in that I've never been sacked as a manager. Even at Falkirk I resigned. The pigeons take up all my time. People ask me what I'll do when I retire but I'm happy as a pig in shite when I'm with my pigeons. There's not enough hours in a day for me. I hate gardening. I finally got the wife in the garden last year after 40 years of marriage and it's the best move I've ever made. She can do it now.

In management, the most important thing is to know how to treat players. I have three daughetrs and each one of them is different. My oldest, if I lift my voice, she'll just say: 'Dad, I'm away.' The second oldest will argue right the way down the road; the youngest is one of these weepy-weepy ones; if a dog dies she'll be weeping. Same with players. Make them believe they are better than they are. I build them up. Like John Prentice did when he was manager at Falkirk. I'd be facing up to Willie Johnstone of Rangers and John would say: 'There'll be nae bother offa him today because you'll have him in your hip pocket.' And it worked.

ALEX TOTTEN: One Saturday night Sergei Baltacha was on the phone to me: 'I'm not happy with you, you swear at me.' Years later he was manager at Inverness and he rang up and told me: 'I know now why you swear at me!'

DAVID MOYES: We all follow in Sir Alex's footsteps; he's the one who started it all off, but you can go back through the years to Bill Shankly and Matt Busby, who were excellent managers. We have a great track record with managers in Scotland, men who have always been really passionate about the game and desperate to do well. A lot have had to move away, and there's some at big clubs and some at smaller clubs – Alex Totten, Terry Christie and Alex Smith done a great job and are continuing to do good things for Scottish football.

The other Shankly: Bill was the monarch of Merseyside.
(© *Daily Record*/Mirrorpix)

It's well clichéd you take a bit of everybody when you become a manager yourself and I have enjoyed all my managers even though we have had fall-outs and fights. I look back now and see bits and think, 'Yes, they knew how to get the best out of me,' then others where I have thought they didn't really have a clue.

Society and football have changed. After the Bosman ruling, there was more freedom for players, and agents were more apparent. There were changes in how players wanted to be treated rather than 20 or 30 years ago. Players have more understanding. At one time they would have been made to run until they were sick; now they are asking the scientific reasons why: 'Tell me why this is good for my body. I want to understand why.' It is their right to do so and if you are moving along with the times you have to have the answers.

Sometimes you have to be the one to bring the bad news, but for everyone like that you get one like Wayne Rooney, and that's when you stand up and start thinking, isn't it a great job when you are lucky enough to come across someone with that sort of ability. It used to be in my day you had to be in the first team at 18. If you got to 19 and were not in the first team people began to say you had missed the boat. I would hope any players at my club are pushing to get in the first team at 18 and I want to see as many young players come through as we can.

ALEX SMITH: Every job I take now I say this could be my last swing at it. But this club could be as good as any.

I won one Cup with St Mirren and two with Aberdeen and a League Championship with Stirling and a League Championship with Clyde. I'm younger than Fergie and a lot younger than Bobby Robson. He has been inspirational for me because he has been at it a long time. This is my 34th year in manage-

Cup of cheer: Alex Smith celebrates a momentous Scottish Cup win with St Mirren in 1987.
(© *Daily Record*/Mirrorpix)

ment; he may have been just before. Looking at him he just oozes enthusiasm and a love for football that is an example to everyone. He just oozes optimism and I would like to think I am like that when I talk football.

JOHN LAMBIE: Some players you have to boot them up the backside, others you can't. Kevin McKee was a quiet lad and you couldn't shout at him. I used to put him on Davie Cooper if we played Rangers and he never gave Davie a kick. Others, like Chic Charnley, you have to bawl at.

I've kicked hot tea in players' faces just through temper. John McNaught, God rest his soul, he was sat there one match at half-time with a cup of tea in his hand reading a programme. Reading a programme! And I just went over and wham! Nobody else ever did that again.

I still say motivation is the most important thing. Knowing your players, too. Like Jock Stein you'd know their wives' names, where they lived, their kids' names.

Football has been my life. People don't know what being a football manager means. You can be sat having your breakfast, or your dinner, and the phone never stops. You never get two minutes' peace. But I don't regret it. I've never had a dull moment and if I died tomorrow I would die a happy man. When I was young my dad was earning £8 a week for being a fireman down a pit and I was getting £12 a week for playing football so that shows you.

ALEX McLEISH: At Rangers I have had to change my ways of working but the important thing is that you never lose your humility.

IAN WILSON: I have had maybe six months outside of football in 26 years.

At Peterhead we have progressed really well, hence the recognition the club got for BELL'S Manager of the Year, but that was for everyone and people stand up and take notice of that. For a small club like us to be challenging Morton for the Championship in the last game of the season in front of 9,000 to 10,000 people was just incredible. It was one of the proudest moments for anyone connected with the club. As a manager, I take it seriously. I want to work at the highest level I can. I did have a chance to go to Inverness Caley, but I had a great relationship with the chairman at Peterhead and I didn't think the time was right. Peterhead fans are passionate with high expectations, which is an indication of how well we have come on in many ways.

Managing is next best thing to playing, but football is always in our lives, we live round football. Tracey never complains, never says anything about it, but from now on, in July, every Saturday is taken. We can never ever have a weekend away and can never go out on a Friday night because if I ask my players not to do it I never do it myself. If I was out on a Friday and we got beat on a Saturday then I would blame myself. It interferes with family life but we have been all over the world. I take the game home and must be a bit hard to live with, but by Monday I am OK again.

TERRY CHRISTIE: At Meadowbank in season 1983–84 I established them in the First Division and we had a super team and there was one point when we were close to being the best team in Edinburgh. I had Darren Jackson in the team and Alan Watts and even though Hibs and Hearts were so well established people still came to see us. But it became a slog staying in the First Division and when Bill Hunter came on the board, a very ambitious man, he put a vote of no confidence in the manager, so I left. Something similar happened at Stenhousemuir. They got better, got a stand and then the directors got ambitious. I could see that coming and I was offered the job at Alloa so I went to Alloa.

JOHN LAMBIE: Most directors don't know much. We were in the Station Hotel with St Johnstone after the League Cup final and one of them blamed me for losing a goal because the Celtic player had a No. 11 on and I had No. 2 on and I was supposed to be on him. He was a midfielder, it was Bertie Auld, but I was supposed to be marking him! I nearly banjoed that director.

5

FACES IN THE CROWD

WILLIE McKIE: Cardew the Cad* was an Alloa supporter, although I don't know how it started. From time to time we would get a letter from him. No real connection, just one of those things, and he never gave an explanation for it. But it's amazing the support we have in London, America and Australia – probably people who moved away.

IAIN PAXTON: At internationals in the Five Nations in countries like France I would be asking journalists if they had heard the Raith Rovers score because there was no other way of finding out. I don't think the French papers would carry it.

Rovers went through a fantastic period, got their chance in Europe and they were even beating Bayern Munich 1–0 in the Olympic Stadium and there is a famous picture of the scoreboard showing that, of course. Everything looked great and they were making money. They had passed the criteria for the Premier League and although Stark's is not the greatest stadium, it's nice enough and they could hold 10,000 – so it fitted the criteria. But like a lot of other clubs they spent all their money doing it and to

---

* Cardew (the Cad) Robinson, stick-like and buck-toothed English radio and TV comic with no previous discernible interest in football.

hold on to players was impossible. Then they lost their manager and really they have never got close to that since. That never stops me supporting them, of course.

CHARLIE REID: It's said about Chelsea in England that a lot of celebrities go and watch them and the same accusation has been levelled at Hibs. But Dougray Scott and Irvine Welsh were Hibs fans long before they were famous. Hibs have always been the outsiders' team in Edinburgh, maybe because of their historical Irish connections, but in my humble opinion people of more imagination support them. Imaginative and artistic people follow Hibs and Celtic.

PATRICK BARCLAY: I live in London, but I still support Dundee from afar. I was at Hampden for the Cup final but it is very difficult to remain a supporter when you are doing my job. For a start you are always working on a Saturday and for another thing you develop a more analytical way of looking at things, which does take some of your fandom away. It takes away a bit of the 'my-team-right-or-wrong' syndrome. Before I ever worked as a football writer and was working as a sub-editor and the kids were growing up we used to take a holiday in August. We were living in Manchester and I worked out that if we had a holiday in one of the glens north of Dundee – they used to play the League Cup Wednesday and Saturday in four-team groups – I could see Dundee five times in a fortnight. So we would all head up to Glen Cova or somewhere like that. I would disappear every three days and leave the kids with my wife. But once you become a reporter that option is lost to you; can't be there when they are playing, although occasionally I have found ways round that. Three years ago they went on a winter break and it was Claudio Caniggia's time and for the first time since coming to London some of the people down here were starting to sit up and take notice of Dundee FC. So I thought I would do a piece on the Bonetti brothers and the Marr brothers, but Caniggia was the catalyst. Now this was typical Dundee because they were having a winter's break in Italy and it was even colder than Scotland in January. We went to this windswept, out-of-season holiday resort near Rimini and it was freezing. But I got an interview with Claudio and that was wonderful.

I liked Bonetti, it was nice to meet all the people at the club and at 1,800 words it was maybe the biggest piece I wrote that year. They had a nice picture of the Tay Bridge and a picture of Caniggia. Talk about a labour of love. When it came to the Cup final in 2003, I asked the boss if he wanted me to go up and help Roddy Forsyth with a supplementary piece to go with his match report – a sort of highbrow colour piece. And to my absolute joy the boss said: 'Hey, come on, I know you, you want to go and enjoy yourself up there, you don't want to be in the press box.'

Too right! I had a great weekend.

The result didn't spoil it at all. I think supporting Dundee has taught me the tricks of being a football fan: not to get as depressed by defeat as you get elated by victories. That is what being a football fan is all about and supporting Dundee has been perfect for that because you get loads of practice at both.

Supporting the national team is even more character-building. I wonder sometimes if it would be nice to support one of the really big teams. There are a few like me. Hugh McIlvanney supports Kilmarnock but I am not sure if he supports Killie with the passion I support Dundee and he certainly doesn't give as much lip about his team as I do. It was the Cup final that made me realise why I love Dundee and have never supported a big team. You look at Celtic, Chelsea and Manchester United fans and they are always so miserable. They just can't take it. I was in Seville with Celtic: 80,000 Celtic fans and, don't get me wrong, a nicer bunch of fans you couldn't meet, but not one of them could see that Porto had tanned their backsides, beaten them fair and square. They were going on about this and that, and it's simply because they were not used to losing. Whereas 1–0 at Hampden against Rangers, for two minutes maybe I was a wee bit glum and then I went down into Glasgow, had a beer, and had a good craic with the Dundee fans.

So let them have all their success and their trophies and all that, but nothing will ever make them less miserable. Manchester United fans, they are spoiled and sated and they will never be happy. I'm happy supporting Dundee.

CHARLIE REID: I confess that I got disillusioned with Scotland after 1978 – I know it was a long time ago – but no one seriously expected us to win the World Cup that year. But there was a cavalier approach and they let an awful lot of people down.

Someone came out with the statistic that the crop of players coming through now is taken from the smallest pool of players that Scotland's had and that's because the laddies at 21 or 22 were at school at the time of industrial action by Scottish teachers. But you can't just blame that. Ireland produces young talent in a lot of sports, not just football, and even Wales have got a good side at the moment. It's very, very disheartening and you just have to hope that in the next decade we get some of that quality back. A lot of Scottish people get their national pride through their football and rugby teams and they have not been great for a number of years now. Nothing stirs the passion more than supporting your own nation, but when that nation doesn't come up to scratch for season after season it gets very sad. It's getting like following Hibs; you expect them to be bad.

I think Scots function better as underdogs; it's part of the national characteristic and it concentrates their minds and brings out the latent aggression and never-say-die attitude. Put it this way: the Scots could never be the Germans. If anything they are more like the Spanish. There's a mixture of the intellectual and inspirational but emotionally we side with the inspirational. Maybe we shouldn't but that's the way we are.

FORDYCE MAXWELL: For football fans it's usually a triumph of hope over experience and by definition most fans are going to be disappointed. You go along and hope for the best and sometimes you get a good result which makes it all worthwhile. It maybe sums it all up for Berwick that last season in the Second Division, because there are only ten sides, they could actually have been either promoted or relegated quite late on in the season. From the time I was 15 to when I reached 30 it was hard to realise what an important part of my life football was, how much I used to enjoy playing and watching. As you get older that fades a bit but it's still there somewhere. The saddest thing is when someone identifies so closely with a side that a bad result has an effect on the rest of the week or even the rest of their lives. I've gone through it myself and there are things in my football-supporting career I cannot explain. Like in the late '60s I started supporting Leeds United and I can remember when they lost the Cup replay to Chelsea in 1970 I was absolutely devastated. But looking at Leeds now I can't for the life of me explain why I felt that way.

Berwick I can explain because they were my local team and I think fans can identify with players of that standard. Most of them think they can do as well as some of the players on the field. It's a couple of miles from where I live now and I can walk to Shielfield, enjoy the game and walk home afterwards. It's the homely aspect of it.

At Berwick there are players getting maybe £50, £60 or £100 a week and down at Newcastle there's some on £40,000 a week, and why the hell should I care? Why should I let myself get so involved that I get depressed if Newcastle lose? You just don't have the same identity with them as the '60s when you would have a guy like Len White running his heart out for them, the only club he ever played for. And Newcastle have two or three right tearaways playing for them. They are great players and I admire their skills but I look at them and say: 'Well, as a person I think very little of you, so why should I get involved?'

It's your emotions. There I am, a middle-aged man sitting watching at Berwick, a so-called sensible person, and they score and you find yourself on your feet with your arms in the air shouting. I can't explain it, can anyone? The only conclusion you can draw is that there is no logic in it.

CHARLIE REID: When people say to me Celtic had a few bad years I think: 'Yeah, well, your bad year is finishing fourth in the league and not making it to the Scottish Cup final. Our bad years are getting relegated, going 20 games without beating Hearts or almost going bust.'

Nobody who follows the Old Firm has any conception about what it's like to follow a team that does not win. I'm not saying it's a cross to bear supporting Hibs, it's not. It's my choice and if I wanted to support Celtic I would go and do it. But it's not my team, it's not my heritage. Celtic and Rangers are tremendous clubs but their conceptions of failure relative to ours are a joke. But there again, Hibs' conception of failure relative to Albion Rovers, say, is also a joke. In the next ten years, however, clubs like Albion Rovers have a far better chance of surviving than Hibs or Hearts have because they don't pay the big wages out, they work on very low levels of income and they survive because there is no huge investment put in. In many ways that is the best way to be involved in sport; it's a community thing instead of just hunting glory all the time. Hibs and Hearts have had no options over the last few years. Fans of small clubs have my greatest admiration; it's rough following Hibs; it must be even rougher following Alloa or someone like that.

HUGH WALLACE: Queen's Park are notorious for their fanatical support, in particular, Trombone Man, who was arrested at Morton and told he had an offensive weapon with him. There is a hardcore of 30 who go everywhere and they give the referees a hard time but they also are totally loyal and at the end of ridiculous matches Queen's Park have thrown away they will still stand and applaud the boys. Some of the other fans spread out a bit, not wishing to be identified with that group, whose choice of language can be a bit colourful.

There's an 80-year-old lady, Ivy Riddell, who is always immaculately dressed and every Saturday she will either make her way to Hampden or early on to the bus to Gretna or Peterhead or wherever her team are playing. She is fanatical about Queen's Park, win, lose or draw, and quite often it can be lose, draw, lose, lose, lose, and she will still be there.

I find that an incredible expression of commitment and loyalty and, yes, fanaticism. But they enjoy it, there's a camaraderie and banter with away fans and away fans can quite often be in single figures. The away fans at Queen's Park will be in triple figures.

This is the third venue for Queen's Park. Before Hampden was Cathkin Park and before that a bowling green. They have been extremely successful, there is a history and on the programme there are achievements starting in 1890 or whenever.

There are supporters' clubs all over the UK and all over the world. I was looking at the website and someone from Sarajevo had logged on. There is something romantic about it, a bit eccentric, too. They are the only amateur club in mainstream football in Scotland and at the end of every season they are going to lose their players. Even in the Third Division a little bit of money is better than nothing and unless they are a Ross Craven or a Danny Ferrie, whose heart is embedded in the club, and they have another career, they are going to move on. A lot of players who have made it elsewhere have touched on Queen's Park – Alex Ferguson and Derek Parlane for example. There are lots of them and we are trying to see if Beckham played here at any stage. He could have been in disguise in a haircut, of course.

In terms of passion and loyalty and commitment there is a great similarity between following football and faith in Jesus. Interestingly, more people go to church on a Saturday in Scotland than go to football on a Saturday, but you get more column inches on the back pages of the papers than the highlights of the services. When fans talk about football as a religion I see that as a challenge to the church to say to people that there is something deeper and richer and a place where everyone is a winner.

BOB CRAMPSEY: Crowds used to be much more disciplined. A lot of them were or had been in the services and the bulk of the rest in craft apprenticeships. If someone let off a volley of swearing, someone else would say: 'Quiet, there are weans here.' And if they did it again: smack. No messing. Even as youngish men people tended to go with father or uncles. The seed corner of the game is the father and his two boys and I don't think we will get that back.

People used to marvel at folk standing out on the terraces with the rain bucketing down, but it was not much different from their houses in many cases. Someone would always be lighting a cigarette and you could see the twinkling lights in the crowd. We used to collect cigarette cards and there was a graduated value for them. The most valuable were the ones with Raich Carter and Stanley Matthews. Manchester United were small beer in those days. Wills and Players would do warships, cricket, football, all sorts of things. Trains they would do. Then, in 1939, they came out with an eagerly awaited new line of cigarette cards: air-raid precautions.

I would never say everything was great in those days. The game has come on a great deal, particularly in the set-pieces; you couldn't bend the old leather ball. Up until 1960 one of the things was how well the centre-forward did against the centre-half. The whole game was a series of duels.

DAVID MOYES: Being a manager now, watching football is as much a hobby. Part of my job is watching games and at least six days a week are football-orientated.

We come up to Scotland and watch a lot of games there; Scotland is my home and I am very patriotic. Down here, I am working with a lot of English people but to be fair they are very well aware of the importance of Scotland, whether it be players or managers in the past, now, or in the future.

GORDON SHERRY: On the Challenge Tour it's difficult to get a Saturday off for a game, but I wanted to support the club, so I have bought a season ticket again. Kilmarnock finished fourth last season and their attendances were way down. They are encouraging kids now with special offers for season tickets and that's the way forward, I think. They need to get bums on seats again. It's expensive; who wants to pay £17 to watch Kilmarnock play Dundee United? It's a lot of money, especially if you have a couple of kids. And it's all PlayStations and computers now. Thomas has one; it was his birthday not so long back and my brother gave him a Kilmarnock goalkeeping top and my mother gave him some goalposts and a net. His PE report from school isn't very encouraging, but he loves kicking the ball around in the garden and he comes home with the scuffed shoes so he's obviously playing at school. So there's hope yet. Alison has been to one game, that was against Celtic and we won 2–0 so she will have to go again some time. I was at that game with Stephen Gallacher, who is a Celtic fan. Celtic ran out and Stephen turned to me and said: 'That's it, we can't win today.'

Why not? 'Because they are wearing that stupid grey strip and we never win in that strip.' Old Firm fans have rules of their own. Alastair Forsyth is a big Rangers fan and is a big mate of Stevie's so they must have some interesting conversations at night. When I shared with Stevie I used to be on the phone home and Steve would say: 'Ask your dad if there's anything in the paper about Celtic.' Alastair is from Paisley so he should be supporting St Mirren, because I say you should support your local team. The buses that leave the centre of Kilmarnock for Glasgow on a Saturday – it's enough to make you cringe.

Football is a big talking point on tour – mostly about English teams which is rubbish, of course. We don't need to mention 1967 or more recent matches, like the last time Scotland played England at Hampden and won 1–0. They should hold that fixture every year. I have been a Scotland fan down the years but like a lot of other people it has fallen off. There doesn't seem to be the belief any more.

JIM LEISHMAN: With fans it's a love for the true supporter even if the team get beat. They complain like hell, they shout like hell, they moan like hell, but they love being there. And that's football.

ERIC MILLIGAN: To be honest I can't understand why someone would switch allegiance. It never ever crossed my mind to support any other club. I support the institution that is Heart of Midlothian, a wonderful evocative name. Rangers? When they thought up the name of Glasgow Rangers they didn't exactly sit up all night did they? Or Aberdeen Football Club. Wow!

I think Hearts fans do have an ever-so-slight inner conceit and there's a romance about the club. Success is always relative to expectation and that applies in football as much as anything else. At the start of the season they know it's highly unlikely that Hearts will beat Celtic or Rangers on a regular basis, but if they do quite well by the standard of the Hearts then I'll be happy. I suspect if I supported Brechin City or Alloa I would have my own measure for success. If you support Morton you would want to see them beat St Mirren and if Dundee then you want to win at Tannadice when you go there twice a season. All football supporters have their own yardsticks. I take my hat off to people who go to East Stirlingshire on a wet Thursday night, week in week out.

As a young guy, like everyone else I was mad about Scotland's international team and would go to Hampden, particularly when we played England, which we did every season. In the years that have passed my support has waned because they are boring and the players that are picked for Scotland are in my view not international class. Ally MacLeod, Jock Stein and Tommy Docherty when they were in charge would attempt to enthuse Scotland supporters and try and reach out to Scottish community and get them backing the national team. Now we have gone in the opposite direction and have managers who keep stressing the need to be realistic and realise that we are no longer a force in world football, that we are all on a learning curve. But we have been learning those lessons, for nearly 30 years. I would have Tommy Burns as manager instead of assistant and Craig Levein as his assistant because they would certainly enthuse people. Berti Vogts, Andy Roxburgh and Craig Brown have spent too much time trying to be 'realistic'.

STUART COSGROVE: When Muirton closed, in the final game we got beat 1–0 by Ayr United; I cut up bits of the turf, took lumps of stone from the terracing and I still have a whole chest of stuff like that – sachets of sugar with Saints on them. I have strips from every season. I never wear them but I would never chuck them out. This is a fanaticism but it is a positive thing in my life. There are times when I wish they had won things that they didn't win, but by and large the experience of being there, the emotional highs and lows, compensate. I believe there is a fundamental difference between the fans of successful clubs and the fans of unsuccessful clubs. If you read something like *Fever Pitch*, that guy's grief is all about coming second in the Premier League; for St Johnstone that would represent the biggest result in their history. We have the same highs and lows and expectations, but a different register of what highs mean. For us success is getting into Europe and being able to play Monaco; it doesn't mean beating Monaco.

In Scotland, because of the Old Firm, it is very, very difficult to be a fan of a small team and accept that you may go the whole of your life and win nothing. That requires a level of dedication that is hard to comprehend.

ALEX TOTTEN: Football for me is the game. I was playing golf in Portugal, Val de Lobo, and we were walking up the 18th and there was a football pitch and I said: 'Ah, that's the real game.' I saw the nets and the goals and got all excited. I play over-35s and I am the oldest player there. Someone says to me: 'Look at Old Willie, he's 48,' and I am 57. It never leaves you. It's in your blood.

STUART COSGROVE: There are certain things in life you shouldn't change and one of them is a football club. I have always

Suffering with Saints: Stuart Cosgrove.
(© *Daily Record*/Mirrorpix)

been a Scotland fan and it comes in a package as a St Johnstone fan. One fan I know, the only Saints games he would ever miss were the Scotland games in Lithuania or somewhere, and he would be hitching to eastern Europe. A lot of St Johnstone fans are Scotland fans; they see, scary thought, Scotland as their big team.

Everyone has human faults and supporting St Johnstone is like a love affair, or a fantastic relationship, and you look back at its ups and downs and think: that's the person I love, rather than: maybe she could be like Linda Evangelista; St Johnstone and Scotland are like that.

The smaller clubs supply the bulk of the Tartan Army and Perth has always been one of the biggest recruiting grounds. That goes back to when it had a huge railway network; if you went north you had to go through Perth, it was the Crewe of Scotland.

My granddad Jim was a train driver and in those days you got a PT, a privileged ticket, and you got two of these a year and you could travel anywhere in the UK with a relative or family friend. So if there were 6,000 railwaymen in Perth that meant there were 12,000 PTs and of course what they would do was use them for Wembley, so in a period of real deprivation you would find that less people from a more deprived area like the Ayrshire minefields would have less chance of going to Wembley, because they couldn't pay the ticket whereas Perth had a free way of getting there. In Perth there was a Wembley Club in every pub and getting the ticket wasn't the problem – it was about saving up the money in the Wembley Club for the bevvy. If Scotland were playing Peru away tomorrow there would be Perth guys there and a St Johnstone banner.

I don't want to be rational about St Johnstone. Beckham and Cantona have never been in a team that has beat St Johnstone. Beckham's never played us and we beat Cantona at beach football once. I am good at things like that, always finding ways of breaking down the big teams.

JACK McCONNELL: Football is a great relaxation. I don't play any more, I am getting less and less fit for that, but I have turned out for parliamentary teams, although three years ago I started to pull a hamstring quite regularly. I played a lot of five-a-side when I was a teacher and for the parliamentary team against journalists, which is a lot of fun. I started going to Scotland games in 1977 and went regularly for a long time. I am the lucky generation of Scotland fans. I was 13 or 14 when we went to Germany in 1974 and was 17 or 18 for Argentina and in my 20s when we went again to Spain and again to Mexico, and although we never quite made it we were competing with the best teams in the world and were never embarrassed as a national team. I have many great memories about being at some of the great games at Hampden and I was at Wembley in 1979, one of the days that spelled the end of the fixture. I would like to bring it back, it was one of the great sporting occasions. These were great times, the night Scotland qualified for the 1978 World Cup and Joe Jordan scoring against Czechoslovakia. I remember that night because I was a month into my time at university and we were packed into some room watching a TV. It has been amazing to meet some of these guys. I taught with a guy called Alan Cousin and he played for Dundee in their great era and you keep meeting these guys in Scotland with this amazing history. His brother was one of the people who discovered Alan Hansen because he came from that area. They still talk about this fantastic 12-year-old they had spotted locally.

JACK McCONNELL: We had made it in 1974 against expectations probably because Willie Ormond, one of the most under-celebrated managers in Scottish football history, had done such a good job getting Scotland on to the world stage. It was a very emotional occasion and of course everyone denies it individually, but the whole country had gone mad believing there was a chance we could win the World Cup and we were comparing the midfield of Rioch, Masson and Gemmill with the others and we were convinced that we were going to take on the world and beat them. It wasn't just that we were going to Argentina, we were going to coast it to the final. Against Holland they proved we had the team capable of doing it, but all the old Scottish faults reappeared – like not being properly prepared. A tragedy, an absolute tragedy, with long-lasting consequences for the confidence of that generation. All of us who went through it are probably still affected by it.

The supporters are probably better balanced now than we have ever been. It was a real trauma the late '70s and through the 1980s.

The excitement of qualifying for the World Cup and somewhere along the line beating England 1–0 with a penalty and believing we were going to win the World Cup and then, of course, it all falling apart. A traumatic thing for so many young Scots. The fans started glorifying the image that had been created. Then there was a bad period and now I think we have reached an equilibrium: win, lose or draw but enjoy the game, even if the team has been shockingly bad, which it has been occasionally, or surprisingly successful. So have a good time and make sure that if the team can't enjoy an international reputation the fans can.

Underrated: Willie Ormond did a great job with Scotland, according to Jack McConnell.
(© The Scotsman Publications Limited)

I met a couple of Icelandic football supporters at the weekend and all they could talk about was Scotland fans. It wasn't just Scotland games but the Champions League final in Glasgow and the atmosphere generated by that game, Celtic fans going to Seville and the general atmosphere created wherever they go. It's very good for the country and the reputation of our country. Other countries' economies also benefit in a certain sector!

BILL PATERSON: My interest in football becomes heightened when you talk about the Scottish international team because that has been ever-present in my life. The terrible traumas of supporting your country. I have lived down in London for over 25 years and while there have never been great nationalist rivalries, they do feel sorry for you if you support Scotland. I watch the big games on television and I love the big occasions, which I suppose makes me a fair-weather fan. I go to the theatre or the movies to see virtually anything that moves, but there is drama in football. If you want a metaphor, in sporting terms, I am the guy who goes to see the big musicals.

WILLIE YOUNG: The passion for football in Scotland is a lot to do with national identity. It's a country that still holds the record for a crowd at a European Cup final. Rangers and Celtic played in Europe on consecutive nights and drew over 100,000 people each, a quarter of a million on successive nights in the same city. The only reason the smaller clubs survive is because of the football club in their community. Who in Britain would have heard of Brechin if it wasn't for the football results? The people who keep these clubs going are remarkable. The nice thing about being a referee and not a player is that you get round to every ground. You see the country and meet a lot of people and you make friends and you remain friends, win, lose or draw.

BILL PATERSON: I was filming in Madrid a few years ago and went to Real Madrid's stadium, what a cauldron of excitement that is. The thing about it is it's so central, in city terms, like Marylebone Road in London or Maryhill Road in Glasgow. Right in the centre of the city, so you get all that seething excitement.

WILLIE YOUNG: Most referees are fans. They are totally committed to football, horrendously committed. There is the training, fitness tests three times a year, meetings, the travel and a family and a job as well, but refs are fans, too. I am a lapsed Scotland fan, but I go to junior matches because if you go to senior matches people tend to jump to conclusions about who you are supporting there.

WILLIE McKIE: You could maybe use the phrase that if you opened us up we would be black and gold inside. Across the board in the lower divisions it's about a love of the game and, in particular, a love of the club. There's a guy called Willie Frederick who is 94 and he saw Alloa win a Championship in 1921–22 as a ten-year-old and he saw the one in 1997–98. He has been BELL'S Fan of the Month and until recent times went to every game home and away.

It has certainly caused a few disagreements with the wife. Something about this game of football does something to your head. It is just unique. I wish more people would follow their local team, and not just Alloa, across the whole spectrum. Clubs like ourselves, it's a struggle financially.

SAMMY THE TAMMY: I am a Scotland fan although I never go as Sammy the Tammy. I had a fantastic four-day trip to Belgium, and there were 14,000 Scots in the Grande Place. I was taking pictures and all the riot police were there because, of course, England had been there the year before. We went up to some of them and asked if we could get a photo of us being arrested and they said: 'Yes, no problems with Scottish fans.' My mate takes a pic of me with the cuffs on, being bundled into the van. We drive off and after a bit I thanked them for their cooperation and asked them to take the cuffs off. 'Oh, no, we go to the station. We do not have keys for the handcuffs.' Thanks a lot, boys. Even after we got beat in the game the banter was starting before we went down the stairs: 'Tokyo, Tokyo, we're the famous Tartan Army and we didn't want to go.'

LAURA HIRD: I wrote a short story once about the funeral of a Hearts supporter. He died after a car crash and all his friends, Rangers and Celtic supporters as well as Hearts, were getting ready to go to the funeral and it's all about the different banter in the pub. They drink in the Tynecastle Arms, which is my local. It's a Hearts pub but run by Hibs supporters, which I find quite healthy. I really enjoy the banter. The manager and manageress get ribbed all the time by the Hearts fans, but it's a real mix. There are Old Firm fans there, too, all having a great banter about football. If there is any aggro it's usually between two Hearts supporters or two Hibs supporters and it's very rarely about football! It's like an escape; they can't escape in any other way than to gather in a big group and talk obsessively about football. They devote eight hours of a Saturday to nothing but football. They talk about nothing else, discussing every move that took place in the game and analysing it. I also find that if they are watching TV in the pub someone will pick up something the commentator has said and it will go round the pub, all carrying on as if they have just thought of what the commentator has said! The day Hearts won the Cup we watched it in the pub and there's these great macho men crying and cuddling each other. A few friends went across to Glasgow and it took so long for it to sink in, it had been so long, they didn't know the shouts and songs for victory. They came back to the pub and the bus dropped them at the end of Gorgie Road. When they walked down the street the houses just emptied and they carried on as if they had just won the Cup! Ken Stott, the actor, comes up from London to the Tynecastle Arms, if he's not filming; he's just an ordinary punter and mixes and joins in the banter and I think 'Good for you'.

GEORGE ORMISTON: It is just part of your life; I think it has involved mine so much I would think my wife could sit here and answer all these questions!

HUGH WALLACE: At Hampden you can have Queen's Park playing Peterhead one week and Zidane on the same pitch the next. That's football for you.

JOHN HUGHES: They're great people in Falkirk, they really are and they take you to their heart if you give them 100 per cent and any player that I bring in, I say that to them: 'You give these people 100 per cent, you dinnae have to be the best, you work your socks off and give them and they'll take you to their hearts.'

The atmosphere at Brockville is something special. I have a running commentary with fans when I play on a Saturday and the ball goes out. I can go over and pick it up and it's the same faces that have been coming for years or if there's an old guy at the front I pick the ball up and grab his bonnet and stick the bonnet on or if there's puddles on the track beside the goal I pick the ball up splashing and they're all soaked and they all know it's coming. Hopefully we can take that down to the new place but you do have to move on.

DOUGRAY SCOTT: The simplicity and the beauty of it is what appeals to me about football. And for me it's a father–son thing and how your relationship with your father is developed through watching football in a working-class environment. A lot of it is not said, but through the journeys you make with your father going to football matches, it's a bonding exercise and it's an act of love between my father and me and the game is so exciting because you know anything can happen. These days it's much more predictable in Scotland because you know Rangers and Celtic are so far apart from the others, but having said that there's still a chance that your team might win on the day and there's nothing that fills you with more sort of excitement than seeing a goal being scored. You get lost in it and it's a great leveller because everybody who's watching football is completely focused on what's going on; you forget yourself and anything that's happening in your life at that time is overtaken by what's going on in the field and football from that perspective is an extraordinary sport, more so than any other sport. I love playing golf, but it doesn't have the same kind of effect on me as football.

It's extraordinary in Scotland – the difference of the grounds, and the atmosphere.

I get recognised at Hibs matches, of course, but I'm just a fan there, a punter. They know I'm a bona fide Hibee.

Scotland played incredibly well against Germany but that's kind of almost like a flash in the pan. I think it's incredibly difficult for Berti Vogts because he's involved at a time in Scottish football that is detrimental to the health of young players really. I mean, you can't expect the team to do well in international football when the domestic clubs are not giving the young players a chance. That's where talent starts; talent starts at a very young age and it has to be nurtured and given the chance. There are plenty of young players on the books of Scottish clubs but they are much more inclined to go for a foreign player who's going to be just playing for the money. They don't play for the jersey and that is why I like Ferguson so much because he's brought through so much indigenous talent at Man United. It's very easy to slag off Man United, but he's the most successful at bringing through young British talent. People should be thanking their lucky stars that there is an Alex Ferguson because if there wasn't they wouldn't have a decent England team.

I'm not saying that foreigners shouldn't come to this country, of course they should but you've got to restrict the amount who come because otherwise you're never going to discover the young talent. If you've got a situation where you've got to work with what you've got then young players who are talented will then get the chance. It's sad, because you know there is talent. But gone are the days when we can have an Archie Gemmill, a Graeme Souness and a Kenny Dalglish all in one team.

JOHN HUGHES: After working so hard all week and taking banter from your mates, you're in your house at the weekend and you're up in the morning and you get your scarf on, go for a couple of pints and go and watch the football. It just takes over, it just gets in your blood and it's in my blood, I never get sick of it.

ALLAN GRIEVE: When I was at secondary school I got into the habit of collecting programmes from all the games and I've got to say I was never very impressed with Stirling Albion's programme. I fancied myself a wee bit as a kind of football writer or something so I wrote to the club with some suggestions on how they should improve their match programme. A couple of days later I got a phone call back from Bob Shankly, who was the club's general manager, saying could I come down and see him; so down I went and that was me, I was now in charge of the club's programme, with a complete free rein to do what I liked with it. So I started writing the programme in the mid 1970s and I've been doing now for more than 25 years.

You're supposed to be diplomatic but sometimes you can make clever use of language, get your point across and claim that people are misinterpreting it. There have been a few times, mainly when I was fairly new to it and a bit young and impetuous.

That I got into a wee bit of bother about some of the things I would write.

It did become a bit of a soapbox and an opportunity to slag off some of our local rivals.

I don't count East Stirling in that. Falkirk are still traditionally Stirling Albion's great rivals but they tend to have been playing in separate divisions; Falkirk have been in higher divisions since the 1960s, so we've had very few local derbys with them in that time. Alloa became really our biggest local rivals in the sense that we were often in the same division as them and Alloa is only six miles from Stirling, so that became probably the biggest grudge match. Stenhousemuir as well; there has never been much love lost between Stirling Albion and Stenhousemuir, although Stirling Albion always think of themselves as being the bigger club. There's no real justification, it's just because Stirling's a bigger town than Stenhousemuir.

ALEX SMITH: We have 22 full-time footballers, 18 full-time Skillseekers and half a dozen girls full-time. It is all driven by the chairman. He loves the Ipswich model, and went down there and came back very impressed by it. So we are getting a new medical area, a new gym and a new indoor-soccer facility. It is a traditional football club with a great set-up and is for the development of players and the entertainment of the local people. People drive down here from the north 70 or 80 miles for the coaching. From Dingwall to John O'Groats is the size of Austria and parents bring them down twice a week. We have community officers out there and we have the second-highest average crowds in the First Division, only behind Falkirk. In Dingwall there are only 8,000 people and our average gate is 3,500, which is fantastic. With Inverness they have two First Division sides in one area and a lot of fans will go and see both on alternate weekends.

ALLAN GRIEVE: Over the years I did whatever needed to be done for the club, I suppose. I got involved behind the scenes in a lot of administration work with the club's managers. First with John Brogan when he was manager in the late '80s and early '90s, and then with Kevin Drinkell in the mid '90s, and I was doing all sorts behind the scenes, including looking after the kit and looking after young players. For four or five years I was actually in the dugout on match days as the kind of coordinator, out there with the substitutes' boards and so on. There's not much I haven't done at some point for the club. On occasions I've substituted for the physio. I've fixed the floodlights and put the weedkiller on the terracing, I've lined the pitch, and even at one point had to fill in as substitute for the reserves.

That was back again in the early '90s when we struggled to get 11 players together for reserve games. We were getting triallists and so on from anywhere sometimes just to make up a team, especially for away games on a Monday night, at the likes of Dumfries or Stranraer, and there were actually two occasions – once at Queen of the South, once at Stranraer – where we were so short I had to be named as a substitute on the team sheet for the reserves. As I say, I would only have gone on in the direst of emergencies. Oh, I had the kit ready to go on. In fact at Dumfries I was the only person in the dugout; everybody else who was there with Stirling Albion that night was playing. I was the substitute, the manager, the coach, the physio, the lot.

Our chairman is a guy called Peter Mackenzie and Peter played against Stirling Albion in Stirling Albion's very first match in 1945. Peter was playing for Airdrie at that time and he did later sign for Stirling Albion for a short spell. He's a local businessman who, over the last 12 to 15 years, must have put in something like £1.2 million of his own money into Stirling Albion with no realistic prospect, I don't think, of getting much of it back. It is just to support the club and keep it going and everybody owes him a huge debt.

We obviously have a hard-core of really keen supporters who muck in and do anything for the club that's necessary, but Peter Mackenzie is the man with the money who has supported the club through really difficult times and has kept the club afloat.

BRIAN FLYNN: Falkirk is such a well-loved club and it is almost part of people's lives. It's more than just a team you go and see on a Saturday – it's a focal point, a social focal point, for so many people. You meet the same people at the same part of the terrace every week. The heart went out of football when they made everybody sit down, it really did. I think Aberdeen were one of the first Scottish clubs to say, 'We want standing.' Aberdeen said, 'Let's go back, let's take a step back.'

Football has changed completely and unfortunately not for the better. My young daughter is really interested and she goes along, but it's not the same; it won't be the same. Having said that you go to some of the grounds where you are all in the one area and it's a great atmosphere.

Stirling Albion and Stenhousemuir are also very, very steeped in the local community. East Stirling is a different animal at the moment because it's so, it's so much on its uppers. Stenhousemuir historically were never allowed to have an overdraft and they were very, very tightly run financially but the social club always did really well and made money all the time. Stirling Albion have a similarly small fanbase but potentially it still is a big area and they could do much better.

I think the bottom line is that Scottish football, even football in general, is going to have to have a really close look at itself and decide where it's going, because the players can't keep taking the money that they are taking at any level, whether you're on 20 quid a week at East Stirling or 20 grand a week at Manchester United. I think clubs have got to live within their budgets and Falkirk have shown that that's possible; get your expenses sorted out, wages sorted out and the rest, with a club breaking even and making a small profit . . . then you know you can't go wrong. If the business is doing well you've always got money to reinvest.

ALLAN GRIEVE: At this school Falkirk may be our local rivals but I really respect the kids who support Falkirk, their local team. There are a lot of Rangers supporters and a few Celtic supporters as well but I'm glad to say the majority of the kids do support Falkirk. I must say I have never tried to convert them to Stirling

Albion because you're born to support a team and I don't think you could ever change.

What I would say, teaching at Falkirk High School, is that I have never yet come across an East Stirlingshire supporter, not one. I am tempted to say, having gone to a few games there, I've never come across an East Stirlingshire supporter there, either. Seriously, I really admire the hundred or so people who are hard-core East Stirlingshire supporters. You know they didn't win a single home game last season but they've still got a hundred or so people who follow them week in, week out, and that's real dedication.

Alloa in recent years have probably been playing above their natural level, you know they've been up in the First Division a couple of times and that's probably above where they really should be. That's down to good management – they've got a superb manager in Terry Christie.

RICHARD GORDON: I've got to meet and know practically all of the Gothenburg team. And that is just such a thrill. I work regularly on the radio with Willie Miller, just a legend, and the thought of me sitting there chatting about football with Willie Miller is just mind-blowing. One thing I would say is that the fantastic thing about all the guys I have met is that they're all really good guys and you can have a laugh with them. Only yesterday I was involved in Football Aid, who hold these games across the country for charity, essentially allowing the fans to live the dream. You've gone on the internet and you've paid for a particular shirt and they had asked me just to help out and publicise it. So yesterday I was playing for Aberdeen. You get away teams and home teams and we were home and these were all fans who had bid for the shirts, so they turn up at the grounds, go into the dressing-rooms, shirts are hanging up with their name and number on and they all walk side by side on to the pitch and play the game. Jim Bett was guesting for our team and Neil Simpson was guesting for the other team and I was kind of pinching myself during that game. Neil and Jim I know very well but they again were two of my heroes from the '80s, and to think, here I am playing at Pittodrie with my heroes. Jim Bett passed the ball to me and I tackled Neil

Simpson once and won the ball! I still feel like I am just a little boy when it comes to football. It's great to get to know these guys on a professional level, having been in the stands for years and years, it's just a fantastic privilege and one that I will never ever take for granted.

Supporting a club is less tangible now than it was. When I first started supporting you could be pretty sure the players you were watching one season you would still be watching the next and the next. When Arthur Graham was at Pittodrie he was there for nine or ten years; Bobby Clark spent practically his whole career there. Even in the 1983 team of Miller, McLeish and Leighton, these guys put in huge spells but if you were to ask me to name the Aberdeen team who won the League Cup final trophy in 1995, the last trophy we won, I could probably come up with seven or eight of them with certainty but I'd struggle with the rest. Now the players are much more transient. For fans it's the memory and the feeling you get when you go through the gates and up the steps; the first game of the season and you go into the stand and you see the pitch and it all comes flooding up.

PETER DONALD: Most of the people who run clubs are fantastic people. When I was at the junior cup final yesterday I was speaking to a man whose name is Arthur MacDonald, who used to be a class-one referee and then he became secretary of the East of Scotland juniors and he now helps with a wee boys' club at Livingston. Arthur is just an example of the thousands of people who spend their lives working in football on a voluntary basis.

You couldn't possibly pay all these people for the work they do, but it's a lifestyle thing, it's not just a wee hobby, it's a lifestyle thing. You talk about the people at Alloa – George Ormiston and Willie McKie, they spend their lives keeping the club going; I remember back in my days my father used to have the games each Saturday and on a Sunday morning he would drop my mother at church, then he would go back up to the junior park where the committee would meet and then they would work on the terraces. That's what these people still do.

The League is professional, or semi-professional football, but the perception of football nowadays is the mega rich – the Celtic, the Rangers. The reality is people putting their own money into the clubs.

I think the Scottish Football League still offer the link between communities and football, which is sometimes not available at the very highest level. I don't mean that Premier clubs aren't accessible to fans, but I think Rangers and Celtic have different institutional status to community clubs. Some of the Premier clubs can still identify with the part of the community – Kilmarnock come to mind – but size is everything. If you look at Alloa or Brechin or Stranraer, they're utterly the focus of the community in the sporting sense and in lots of other ways. At the top level of football sophistication has replaced enthusiasm and I have to say that I feel more comfortable at this level than I do at the very highest level. I like high-quality football, but in Scotland it is the people's game. We are almost a one-sport nation in terms of it being the focus of the community. We had Brechin City into the BELL'S Cup final this year and that's absolutely fantastic. The number of people who turned out for Brechin in terms of the size of their population is quite incredible.

If you look at Morton, a club who were on the edge of oblivion, and that's not exaggerating, they were going down the plughole, they came back and in one year have got promotion and on the last day of the season get 8,500 people to come and see them play Peterhead.

That's what a good club properly run with a focus in the community – and one giving the community a chance to feel a part of the club – can do. It was the supporters who actually took them through their bad times and raised money so I think these are real qualities that I don't think you can say apply in other areas of business.

RICHARD GORDON: More than ever now though, and I'm sure a lot of fans would agree, the club means more to us as fans now than it does to players. I think at one time the players would have shared that bond. I think it's much less likely that players do hang around for a few years and build up some sort of relationship with the fans. It's difficult for a player to come in and immediately strike up a bond, although it happens from time to time.

You do at a lower level, at the Alloas and places like that. It's a financial thing, I know, but even at the lower clubs – and I keep a fairly close eye on the lower divisions so I know what is happening for my job – the start of the season is a nightmare because it's like half the players have moved on, moving around the clubs. It's usually a couple of months into the season before it settles down enough for you to go, 'Oh, he plays for them and he's moved to there.'

PETER DONALD: For me football is a game that is best enjoyed by playing it, and obviously you can't do that all your life so you have to find another way of enjoying it. Most people start off by having played the game and enjoying it and after that you find a club and go and support your club. I think it gives people a social focus that they can take through their life, they can enjoy the commitment and the camaraderie of their club. It's not somebody else's club, it's their club and the astonishing thing for me is even

Big league: SFL secretary Peter Donald has seen the commercial side of the game flourish. (© *Daily Record*/Mirrorpix)

with the arrival of foreign players at the top level supporters can still have that affinity with their club even though those overseas players will come and go, because they're not local lads. People feel they're on a journey together.

ALEX SMITH: My brother is a director at Stirling Albion and he is also president of the Football League, but I know the commitment he has to Stirling Albion and the commitment he has to football. There are lots out there like that. They give everything to the game.

ARTHUR MONTFORD: There are great enthusiasts here. The stadium manager is the son of Douglas Rae and he has spent hours and hours locating things like toilets, disabled toilets, putting up proper steps, crash barriers and seats, transforming the place. You have to have that passion otherwise the clubs can't survive. Clubs like Morton exist because of that. In the time I have been supporting Morton I haven't seen a lot of changes in Cappielow, to be honest. The floodlights didn't come in until after the war. We were in the Premier League for a number of years and did very well, under Benny Rooney. But like so many clubs we were victims of the economic pressures of football in the '70s and '80s which made life very difficult for smaller clubs and I think they have done well to get back into the Second Division. I am very hopeful that we might make it two in a row and get promotion.

There are a number of players who are full-time who operate on not-great wages but who put a lot into it and we have a number of part-time players with good jobs who naturally don't want to give them up. For a Third Division club to spend £50,000 on someone like Alex Williams is very ambitious, but that shows the extent of Douglas Rae's ambition and emotion.

PETER DONALD: It's the community element that's where it works best for me. Kids will be impressed nowadays because of television and marketing and sales, it's got to be Rangers, it's got to be Real Madrid, whoever, but that's never been me and this maybe takes me back to where I started. Johnston Burgh is my team and I still keep an eye on the results and if somebody was to ask me who I supported it would be Johnston Burgh.

Fans might not go to a game for ten years, but if their team make a final they will go. Dundee brought 20,000 to Hampden for the Scottish Cup final and Ayr United made it to the League Cup final last year and brought about 12,000 people. When you go back to the next league game they're back to their usual 1,500, but the link is still there and that's what football is for me. It's about your belief in your team. People will go and see success, however relative that is. Hibs, when they were in the First Division, had better attendances than they had in the Premier; you'll get more people coming to see you if you are winning.

Alloa and clubs like that are utterly stretched to be First Division clubs and to raise the funds to get players to keep wee Terry Christie happy, and they will overstretch themselves so they go down a division, regroup and they will have another go. Like I say, it's the journey and not the destination.

CRAIG LEVEIN: At Cowdenbeath the support wasn't great. They were very vocal and they were always behind the team, but it would be in the hundreds rather than the thousands. It's a place I've got very fond memories of, as you can imagine; I played there and I also managed there. There is an important part for these clubs to play in the local communities. Round about January time with Cowdenbeath mid-table and they're away to Forfar, you'd be lucky if you got two carloads of people going up, but you get to stick together, you get a chance of getting promotion and all of a sudden the people and the community are there. So I'm not saying that every week they are an important part of the community, but whenever the club achieves something or looks like achieving something then the community starts rallying round and starts showing their support, and that's not just Cowdenbeath I'm talking about. Everybody becomes proud of the team and also the village or town that they're from and I think that serves a great purpose.

The dedication of some of these people is incredible, as I say we get people who turn out when the team's doing well, but there are those who pride themselves on following their team anywhere no matter if they are winning or losing.

DAVID McGREGOR: Unfortunately, there are no multi-millionaires running Forfar. I run it as a business but it's still a hobby. There are about 20,000 shares issued, but nobody owns the company, nobody owns the club. There are six of us on the board and a very strong supporters' club who over the past 50 years have donated nearly half a million pounds to the club, which is quite amazing. For example, at the end-of-season dance there in May they presented the club with a cheque for £15,000. That's half a year's fund raising. If it wasn't for all these things we'd never be able to survive.

Nobody gets paid here. Stewart the turnstile operator, programme sellers, the girls that do the refreshment kiosk are all doing it for the love of the club. The only ones who get paid are obviously the playing staff and the manager, and we do have a full-time groundsman who is a character in himself. Martin Gray keeps a fantastic ground and also does the kit. He joined us straight from school some 16 years ago and we're just amazed at his kit room and everything and the way he even cleans the soles of the boots, never mind the uppers.

I sometimes wonder if the expectations and hopes of the board are sometimes greater than a lot of the fans'. A lot of the fans at Forfar are more than delighted if they hold their own in the Second Division. The board would love to have another crack at the First Division and in fact in the aftermath of our televised Cup quarter-final against Rangers 15 months ago we spent quite a bit of money building a side for last year and ended up just failing again to get that First Division place. We failed by three points the year before and I think we failed by two this year.

IAN BLACK: The Queens fans are quite loud and seem to make more noise away from home. There's a guy with a drum and a lad with the bagpipes and they usually go to the away games. Certainly they get the crowd going but seemingly at home it's not the same, I don't know what it is. John Connolly, the manager, says the team and the players seem to react better when they are away from home. I've done everything at the club basically. I've even dressed up the club mascot, Dougie the Doonhamer. I've actually painted the stand, mended fences, collected litter and when they are needing a hand I give them a hand. If you want to know what I think about the club, you're maybe better having an interview with my wife, Rosa, as she could probably tell you better. On saying that I go on a Saturday, I take my two daughters – they are both season ticket holders – and my wife goes as well to games.

I look after the museum at the ground, which has a lot of different things, ranging from an original floodlight bulb from the old floodlights to Zico's Brazil top. Many years ago, the chairman of Queens, a chap called Roy Harkness, who was also a prominent local businessman, was presented with the shirt by Zico after a World Cup game in Spain in 1982. Billy Houliston, who played for Scotland in 1949 when we beat England at Wembley, played for Queens and I've got his three Scotland tops and his Scotland cap in the museum. His son Keith is on the board. It's free to get in. You just make an arrangement by appointment and I usually take everybody round, so I am the tour guide as well and I've even been kit man for a night.

DAVID McGREGOR: The good thing about Scotland fans is that everything they do is fairly good-natured. Having been abroad, not on a lot of occasions, but on a few occasions with the Tartan Army, their behaviour at times I often think is not quite as good as it's reported to be. But the good thing about it is, unlike English, German and Dutch fans, it's all fairly good-natured. There are times it would make you cringe as well, but at least it's not troublesome and that's the huge difference.

We've got one fan, Frank Rae, who will be up for his season ticket in two or three weeks. He's 96 years old and he's still at every game, even in the depths of winter. He was brokenhearted a couple of years ago when he had to start sitting in the stand. His son-in-law goes with him to games. He's about 70.

LORD MACFARLANE: I am the patron of Queen's Park although I have to avoid taking an interest in the clubs because the sponsor has to be neutral. But nobody objected at the time.

Football is so much part of our culture as it is really something special for the nation and I've seen a big difference, a big improvement in the Scottish Football League in the last five years. There's a very strong wish to improve the game, to keep the ball on the ground, pass the ball about. Even my wife used to notice that they kicked it from one end to the other some years ago and she recognises the difference in quality.

I'm certain that I'm the only person in football who has been to all the Scottish Football League grounds in one season – we are talking about 30 which are geographically widespread and are really not easy to get to in one season because obviously other commitments arise. Peterhead to Stranraer, Berwick on the other side. Ross County to Berwick then other clubs all over the country. My wife loves Brechin, because Brechin has a beech hedge right down one side. They don't have a wall to stop people coming in down that side, they have a beech hedge, which is amazing. So Brechin, Forfar, Montrose, Arbroath that's the little group that we go to as often as we can and, of course, the clubs like Dumfries and Stranraer, which are a day's march. The only club in the Scottish Football League that has got a sign outside it saying 'Welcome' is Albion Rovers, who have a big sign saying: 'Welcome to Cliftonhill'.

The common factor and the marvellous thing is the people. Many of my wife's friends ask her why she goes to football with me every Saturday. She says because we meet a lot of very nice people. That's a compliment for the clubs that she feels that she wants to come because she gets on very well with the people and the football people are exceedingly nice. There are always rotten apples in anything but in general they are super. As you know they are always marvellously well turned out, they take great pride in wearing their blazers and their white shirts and looking like ambassadors, and club ties; they are ambassadors. That's good as well because keeping standards up in everything is so important in Scotland but keeping football clubs going is a huge task. I'm always saying to business people these days that we've all got big problems, all businesses, as you well know, are difficult, but the main thing is to try to keep the club in existence because if you can keep them in existence then at least there's always a chance they're going to do better, whereas if they go out of existence that's the game up and the same applies to football clubs. Clubs like Raith Rovers, who have come through a bad spell, are back up to the First Division and I'm pleased that Falkirk have done so well. Falkirk are very well supported in the local community, and are now going to go to this new ground.

My wife got more and more interested in the community aspect of the football clubs and she meets a lot of very nice ladies who are along on the same kind of mission as her, to support their husbands and keep the club strong. When we went to Berwick on one occasion, there would be 245 people there and Berwick were having a particularly dull spell during the game and one of the wags in the stand just along from her shouted out: 'Bring on Lady Macfarlane!'

Jimmy Curle, who has just retired as Berwick chairman, has done a super job and he is an agricultural auctioneer, and during foot and mouth no cattle were transported and he had a hard time, but he kept Berwick going even in that period which was a huge personal financial sacrifice. There are lots of them doing that and there is a marvellous book to be written about the clubs and the turmoil that they've all come through because every club's got it at some stage.

CHARLIE REID: On tour at the moment most of the conversations with Craig are about the state of Hibs and that some of the debt was unnecessary. Too much was spent on the two stands behind the goals that cost twice as much as they should have. The agenda of the Hearts and Hibs is to do with business. I will follow Hibs if they move out to Straiton but with deep regret. Not a merged team, however. Who knows? In ten or twelve years I may be moved round if they merged, but I think I would rather go and watch Boroughmuir play rugby because at least they know who they are. There is not one Hibs or Hearts supporter I know who wants a merger. If that is the long-term objective they are going to have to do it in the teeth of fierce opposition from both sets of fans. The support would drift away because that mile radius around Easter Road contains an awful lot of Hibs support; the same in Gorgie. If you lost 20 to 25 per cent of your support over 5 to 10 years, then the pressure would be on and the next step is the merger.

I go and sit behind the goal and take my three sons and, generally, my wife comes along as well. So I am buying five season tickets a year. No matter what the board does, I will support Hibs . . . as long as they stay as Hibs.

FRANK McAVEETY: Scotland gave the game to the world and we have the longest-surviving national trophy, the Scottish Cup; it's the only cup in the world that is still the same cup as it was when it was first created way, way back in the nineteenth century. Football also gave a sense of who they were to many of our communities who were either migrating from other parts of Scotland or from Ulster and the rest of Ireland. They came over to Edinburgh, they came over to Glasgow; and Rangers came from a Highland tradition, Celtic from an Irish tradition and the likes of Hibernian and Dundee United also have a very strong sense of tradition. There are probably few other cities in the world that have three major stadiums.

GORDON BROWN: I have followed Scotland's World Cup fortunes since I was a schoolboy and was one of thousands of teenagers who stayed off school when Scotland had to beat Italy to qualify for the 1966 finals in England, and failed. As a schoolboy I turned to the sports pages long before I turned to news or politics. You start young and you can't give up supporting Scotland. You can't walk out on them simply because they are playing badly. Once disappointed, twice we turn up, and as optimists. Scotland is like that. We have done well in a lot of World Cups, but never well enough. The problem is, Scotland teams carry more than the hopes of football fans, they carry the hopes of a nation.

DOUGRAY SCOTT: Given the choice between an Oscar or a World Cup win for Scotland, I'd go for . . . both!

GEORGE ORMISTON: I have a slightly crazy love for this club.